Christine Brady has considerable insight into coping with change. As founder-editor of *Family Circle* magazine and an established writer she has met and talked to hundreds of readers who have overcome difficulties and dealt courageously with their altered circumstances. When researching previous books she has heard many fascinating stories from the growing army of self-employed men and women of why they branched out and changed their lifestyle.

She has coped with change herself including tackling a shift of emphasis in her career, moving to a strange area, helping her husband through major illness and redundancy and coming to terms with the gap caused by children leaving home.

Christine Brady believes strongly that taking a positive attitude, looking on life as an adventure and maintaining good health, together with interests and hobbies, can make for a rich and fulfilling life whatever one's age.

A CHANGE FOR THE BETTER

CHRISTINE BRADY

CORGI BOOKS

A CHANGE FOR THE BETTER

A CORGI BOOK 0 552 13142 3

First publication in Great Britain

Corgi edition published 1988

This book is set in 11/12 pt Garamond

Corgi Books are published by Transworld Publishers Ltd.,
61–63 Uxbridge Road, Ealing, London W5 5SA, in Australia by
Transworld Publishers (Australia) Pty. Ltd., 15–23 Helles
Avenue, Moorebank, NSW 2170, and in New Zealand by Transworld Publishers
(N.Z.) Ltd., Cnr. Moselle and Waipareira Avenues, Henderson, Auckland.

Made and printed in Great Britain by
The Guernsey Press Co. Ltd., Guernsey, Channel Islands.

CONTENTS

ACKNOWLEDGEMENTS

The list of addresses and map on pages 64–78 and 79 are extracted from *Guide for Applicants for 1988 BA Degree Courses*, © 1986 The Open University, and appears with their permission.

The height/weight chart on page 111 is reproduced by permission of the Health Education Authority.

1
COPING WITH CHANGE

Even at its most consistent, life is full of change. As children we are constantly exposed to new experiences. Because our canvas is almost blank we find it easier to absorb them and revel in the process.

As teenagers we also find ourselves continually facing a different set of situations and relationships. Because of our zest for life and enthusiasm, we go out and look for them rather than wait for it all to happen on our doorstep.

Once into middle years, most of us have settled into a fairly predictable routine. We think we know what will happen and what we will be doing this time tomorrow or next week, and sometimes even next year. When we find this pattern disturbed, particularly unexpectedly, we feel disoriented and uncomfortable. In extreme cases, if the change is sufficiently dramatic, we may feel a sense of panic.

All change, even when it is to our advantage, can make us uneasy. A promotion at work exposes us to different colleagues. We leave behind our comrades who in future will view us differently. If moving to another district is involved, we will uproot our family and leave behind friends and companionable neighbours. If we have teenagers at home, it may trigger off their leaving the nest.

All change, whether it be good or bad, will result in some form of loss. It may be difficult to see what good is to be gained if the sense of loss is all-pervading. Because the loss comes well before any nett gains from the new set of situations, it is easy to become depressed and long for things to stay as they were. By anticipating that you will feel this way you can do a lot to lessen the pangs. On bad days, sit down and write out what the change has helped you achieve. Even in the most dismal situation, something can usually be found on the plus side.

A new location will eventually result in making at least new acquaintances, if not friends. There will be an opportunity to discover a new town with different amenities and you will still have your previous contacts which you can maintain with letters or by phone, and arrange regular or just occasional meetings and visits.

Different jobs bring stimulation and challenge even if they are less financially rewarding or of narrower scope than the one you had previouly. What may appear to be a step down for you in terms of job definition could result in less stress, more time for family and leisure pursuits and a chance to get involved more in the local community.

However tedious and mentally unrewarding a job has been, to be without it can be a great shock. Whether you have given in your notice with the firm intention of doing something that you have planned for months, or even years, or lost your position suddenly, it will be a wrench to discard the familiarity of the routine even if you believe you have detested it for many years.

By knowing that your change from routine will follow this pattern, you can do a lot to minimise the sense of unease. Wherever possible, try not to alter too much at once. Sometimes this is impossible, but it can help considerably if you can tackle one area of change at a time. In a case of bereavement, alas, this is not possible, but this is discussed more fully later on. If too many things in your life are changing at once, the difficulties will be far greater and it will take much longer to rise above them.

Karen resigned from a highly paid, extremely stressful job to launch her own one-man business just weeks before her youngest daughter left home to get married. The previous year her husband had retired from work early because of ill health. Although the couple were cushioned financially, it was still a blow to both of them.

Karen appeared to cope with the considerable change in her lifestyle very well. She kept busy both at work and in her leisure and was still closely involved with her family. But to everyone's astonishment, when her dog died suddenly six months later, she went to pieces. The death and loss of companionship of a beloved pet was just the final straw.

Paul was made redundant after working in the accounts department of a large multi-national company just weeks before his fortieth birthday. It took him over six months of concentrated effort before he found another job of similar status but with quite a lot less money.

During that six months his lifeline was the fact that he was secretary of the local bowls club. Two or three evenings each week and at weekends he was involved in its activities, and it gave him a normal facet to life when everything else appeared to be going from bad to worse.

One of the most important things to do when adversity strikes and you are suddenly left high and dry is to spend only the minimum time wallowing in self-pity. It is beyond the scope of most of us not to rage at what has happened, to vent anger at anyone we feel contributed to the cause, and to feel overwhelmed. That is normal and not really harmful if it lasts just a short time. What is more serious is to allow the feelings to fester and become deeply entrenched attitudes. The secret is to look forward, and salvage any good that can come out of the encounter and to put behind for ever what is bad.

Often it is only years later that you can look back and view trauma in its proper perspective. At the time the anger can etch deeply into your attitude to the establishment in general and very often your family in particular.

At 63 Arthur positively glowed with enthusiasm. At quite the most unfortunate age, 61, he had been made redundant from a large corporation after spending 40 years with them. He had been cocooned, not only in the security of his job and a regular pay packet, but in the comradeship of belonging to a large department, a union to negotiate better terms and a personnel department to turn to for guidance.

It was a rude awakening to find it had all vanished, and he was tipped out into a highly competitive job market in an area of exceptionally high unemployment. But two years later he could say quite positively, 'I wish it had happened years ago.'

Once revived from the shock of leaving the company's cosy nest, he started a modest business, at first from his own home and then from a tiny shop premises in the next street. He offered a service that the 'big boys' no longer provided and became a useful part of his local community. He could say quite honestly that life was good.

What happened to Arthur has happened to many people of various ages in recent years. What made him survive was his optimism and will to succeed, backed up by a supportive wife. He had his problems in raising finance, and wondering if he was capable of doing anything – there's nothing like losing a job abruptly to take away your confidence. He overcame the difficulties, and even better, within two years could say that he was enjoying himself more than ever before.

Mervyn, a 61-year-old, was forced into early retirement after a major illness made him less than fit to carry on in his position. His 'pension' just about paid his paper bill. For several months people around him watched as he settled into the life of a semi-invalid. But gradually, almost imperceptibly at first, he turned the corner and very very slowly regained his health sufficiently to take a part-time job, to rearrange his finances by moving to a smaller house and renew an interest in several hobbies. Now, five years later, he is financially sound, in reasonable health, still interested in his job and has retained his old hobbies. Mervyn's secret was that he didn't waste time looking back. What was done was done and there was no point in going over old ground. It was time to look to the future and make a success of it.

Of course, change is not always outside our own control. Sometimes we take the deliberate decision to make a new start, to alter our lifestyle. This resolve can extend beyond just changing a job or even combining it with a move. It can result in a total alteration in source and amount of income and in attitude to life in general.

Dick was 41 when he decided to leave the 'rat race' and retire from his job. Having trained as a pilot in the Fleet Air Arm, then read engineering for three years at Southampton, he had spent the post-war years involved in helping emerging nations, released from the Empire, in setting up their own air forces.

Those years were hectic, involving endless travel, so much so that he based himself and his family in Beirut during its heyday. In consequence, he made a lot of money, but finally decided he had had enough.

For several years following, he and his family lived in Corfu, travelled a lot, dealt in property and thoroughly enjoyed themselves. But gradually, they all began to think of home.

They moved to southern Ireland where he bought a disused monastery and turned it into an up-market hotel. It was a great success but extremely hard work, so after three years they sold it and moved to Devon.

Devon they found was a disappointment. His wife Anne wanted to move to Kent, which Dick was very much against, as he considered it a dormitory area of London, but they rented a house there long enough to convince Anne that Dick had been right.

They then moved to a small Suffolk village, not far away from where Dick had been born, and they set about converting a small cottage which had a substantial brick outbuilding. All the time he was doing the conversion, Dick had no clear idea of what he really wanted to do. One day, out of the blue, his wife said, 'Why don't you make rocking horses?'

The idea appealed. Dick visited toy shops to see what they had, but found very little. Even top shops couldn't produce anything very impressive. He bought two old rocking-horses, took them to pieces to see how they were made, and from that evolved his own design. It was almost three years before he was satisfied.

There is more to a rocking-horse than meets the eye. Stability, safety and the swing of them are all important, and the size and overall design must appeal to old and young alike. Dick's engineering background certainly helped.

His debut as a craftsman was at the Essex county show where he took a stand, appropriately decked with flags and bunting, and the business was well and truly launched. The local television station gave him coverage, then the Press Association released a feature to over 120 provincial newspapers, and from there business just took off.

Dick's order book at the moment is full for nine months ahead. He aims to make one rocking-horse every two weeks, but in this current year he will make around 40. He has been joined by a young part-timer who does some of the basics.

Disciplined about his work, Dick works regularly from 9am to 5pm each day, in theory five days a week, but he finds his busiest time for callers is at the weekend, when passersby often stop when they see his sign outside the house.

To get an idea of what to charge, he wrote to other makers of rocking-horses for their price lists, but comparing them with the standard of workmanship, was less than impressed. By selling only directly to customers, Dick fixed what he felt was a reasonable price, but sees now that it was too low and has found it difficult to increase his charge.

Each of his horses is numbered and catalogued, and there is a plaque installed bearing the owner's name and any message from the donor. One recent customer bought the horse as a gift to his wife on their thirtieth wedding anniversary. Another single lady lived in a coach-house and thought 'she ought to have a horse'. Two are currently on their way to Italy destined for a home for mentally handicapped children, where the doctor in charge is convinced of the therapeutic qualities the rocking motion can impart to disturbed children.

Although his order book is full, and he is registered with The Craft Council, Dick still gives his business a little extra impetus each year by taking a stand at the local agricultural show.

His advice to people who are faced with change is, 'Don't just think that you should continue to do the sort of things you have been doing already. Take a look at new ground – it will give you more of a chance to see a gap in the market.

'If you take a substantial drop in income, try to accept it as a total change of lifestyle. Be prepared to step into a new role and make it a way of life. Don't keep looking back. Don't have regrets – look to the future as a great adventure. Above all, keep a confidence in yourself and be positive about everything you do.'

Mike was manager of a toy shop where he found he was gradually becoming more and more disenchanted. The small family firm he had joined in the beginning was now a large group, and he found himself increasingly pressured by the memos and management meetings that were required by head office.

A friend of his invited him to join a painting group he was trying to set up locally. The idea was that they should all meet in a room over the pub once a week. Although he had never attempted to paint before, Mike soon found himself hooked. When his friend left the district, he asked Mike to take the class over for the last six sessions, and at the end, the group begged him to arrange a new term.

Before long he was taking other classes and painting in his spare time. Then he took the big decision. His children were grown up, his mortgage paid, and he decided to resign from the toy firm and take up painting and teach art full-time.

His first task was to canvass over 300 homes in his area to see whether he could sketch their houses. In spite of including stamped addressed envelopes, he received precisely one reply.

Not disheartened, Mike resumed painting as often as he could and found then, as now, that most of his work was sold 'on the easel'. People looking over his shoulder are most likely to ask to see the finished work or arrange to buy it there and then.

Ten years further on, Mike now divides his week between twelve hours of teaching and the rest painting and sketching. He considers that the hourly rate for teaching adults is good and it takes care of his basic commitments.

Since he bought a van, which he has fitted out with a small sleeping area, he finds he can get up and go literally wherever he pleases.

With invitations to demonstrate at art clubs throughout his area, and the opportunity to teach at residential centres from time to time, Mike is convinced he did the right thing. Now the pressures of his large firm environment are gone he feels free to do his own thing.

REDUNDANCY

Nothing that anyone can ever say about redundancy can alter the devastating shock when it happens to you. The fact that it is now comparatively commonplace in no way prepares you for the trauma when you are faced with the fact that your livelihood and whole lifestyle are threatened.

When you approach retirement, however much you may have buried your head in the sand and refused to acknowledge it would really happen, you know in your heart that it has to be faced. In redundancy, or if for whatever other reason, a job you felt would continue is suddenly taken away from you, you have to deal with the shock of rejection as well as the more practical matter of what you will do instead.

People react to shock in different ways. Some retreat into themselves and don't wish to discuss the problem at all. Others will rant and rave and vent their anger on anyone who happens to be around, particularly anyone they feel may have had a hand in the matter.

If redundancy plans at your firm are still not official, or if you have not been pin-pointed as one of those on the 'hit list', don't automatically assume the worst. If you belong to a union, it will be negotiating and gathering information on behalf of all its members. If you have a personnel department, it will be making plans, and if it is not keeping you sufficiently informed, you can at least consult its staff on specific queries. It could be, however, that the situation resolves itself. The firm may receive a much needed cash injection, or other vital orders may come through so that the firm can keep going.

What you must now bear in mind is that your job could go and that you must be ready to face that fact. You must start to make plans.

Most likely, your first thought will be to find a job as similar as possible, both in content and salary prospects, to the one you are leaving. You may find that this is a practicable possibility. If you are in an up-and-coming industry where new jobs are being created, it will not be as difficult as if you are in one that is in decline. Similarly, if you are in an accounting function, in whatever capacity, you will probably find several jobs open to you, although the salary structure may not be as attractive.

If you plan to take this avenue of replacing the job you have had with a similar one, go at finding an alternative with all your energy. Don't go about it in a half-hearted way. Competition is keen, and if you work in a large firm that is closing down and a number of people are about to flood the job

15

market, you will need to have a keen edge to make a successful move. Younger people are more likely to slot into new jobs than those in their late forties or fifties, and the chances are better while you are still in employment, so make the most of the time you have left at your firm to examine the job market and write applications.

Personal contacts are usually the best way of finding a new job. The most likely source will be anyone who knows you in your present capacity. It may be your own boss or someone in your personnel office who knows of openings in similar firms. It could be one of your customers, past colleagues or those in similar positions. Family friends with good business connections or those in any local clubs you belong to may be able to help. It's no time to try to keep up appearances and act as though nothing has happened. The more people who know you are looking for a job, the better the chance of someone being able to point you in the direction of a new position. Never give up. Your confidence will have taken a knock but even if you have to put on a brave face when you are feeling terrible, don't look down-hearted while the rest of the world is looking on.

It's a good time to take stock of your skills and experience and examine them in detail. You will need a current curriculum vitae, and it may seem strange at this stage to have to go back to beginnings and put your qualifications and job experience on paper. You may care to consider at this stage whether you want a job that is exactly the same as the one you are leaving. Did it give you complete satisfaction? Were there some parts you liked a lot better than others? Have you developed a skill, perhaps from a hobby or spare-time interest that may lead to full-time earning?

If you have been following a skill such as dress-making or restoring furniture for many years it could serve you well as a new career, even one you may prefer to the rather dull job you are leaving. Perhaps your own on-the-job training, in people management, for example, may lead you to organising a workforce or training young people for specific tasks.

You will never have a more opportune moment than at this time to sit back and examine your skills; not just the ones you started out with in the job twenty years or more ago. Make sure you are seeing the wood for the trees. Your true skills may not be the ones for which you were originally employed. Looking for exactly the same job as the one you had implies that the firm itself saw your true skills and was able to utilise them to the full. Very often this is not so; employers for many reasons may ignore your potential or not have the jobs available to make the most of your skills.

It may help to ask your husband or wife, or someone close to you, possibly a colleague at work or a trusted friend, what he or she thinks. If you have grown-up children, ask them. It can be quite revealing to hear yourself summed up in a few words by a young person in his or her twenties who may be more switched on to the current job market than you are.

What qualities are most needed to survive redundancy – to emerge victorious at the other end of such an encounter? They are the same qualities that are necessary throughout life, so:

* be optimistic
* be realistic
* don't expect too much too soon
* look after your health
* keep an open mind about people and situations.

FINDING A NEW JOB

Your own personal assessment will be valuable when you come to be interviewed by a personnel department or a career consultant or a prospective employer. Each will appreciate the fact that you have presented your credentials in an efficient way and have done some of their own work for them.

While you are job-hunting, take a realistic approach to your chances:

* Don't apply for jobs that specify a widely different age from your own.

* Be positive, think of it as a new beginning, not the end of the road.

* Recognise there will be disappointments and don't let rejection affect you too much.

* Continue to believe in yourself.

Make looking for a new job your major task. Concentrate on it full-time. Prepare the very best curriculum vitae and get professional advice if you think you need it.

Comb the papers for job adverts – you will soon know which day which newspaper concentrates on your particular expertise. Read them in the local library to save spending too much money.

When you apply for jobs, send in addition to your curriculum vitae, a precisely worded letter highlighting why you think you are particularly suited to the job.

Read the job advert very carefully for clues about what is required. You can learn a lot from the way it is worded. If you are invited to write for more details and an application form, do just that. Don't think you will fare better by telephoning and conducting a mini-interrogation there and then.

Contact suitable employment agencies. There will be those that specialise in your type of work, and most large cities will have executive agencies for suitable personnel. Read their terms carefully (see Chapter 2, Ways to Work).

REDUNDANCY ACTION PLAN

1. Get the best advice you can from your own managers or personnel department in the firm. They may be in contact with other local firms who have staff vacancies. Your union or staff association may be able to give you assistance.

2. Make sure you get all your entitlements in terms of redundancy pay and government benefits (see Chapter 8, Managing Your Money). Take advice about your pension rights.

3. Let as many people as possible know you are looking for a job. Tell those of your own friends and neighbours who may be able to give you a lead. Previous contacts through your job may know of vacancies.

4. Prepare a curriculum vitae – you can get professional help with these if you wish. The aim will be to highlight your strengths and gloss over weaknesses without bending the truth.

5. Take a long hard look at what you really want to do. You

may find you would like to use the opportunity to retrain for another job or switch to a completely different lifestyle.

6. Check your finances. If you have a mortgage and wonder how you can carry on payments, contact your building society or bank manager at the earliest opportunity to put them in the picture. If you are paying rent and don't know how you will manage, contact your local office of the Department of Health and Social Security (DHSS) or get advice from the *Citizens' Advice Bureau*.

7. Sit down with your partner, and your children if they are old enough to understand, to explain how the changes will affect them. Even quite small children can be extremely understanding, and it is better to level with them rather than let them feel the tension of the inexplicably cancelled holiday and whispering behind closed doors.

8. Don't spend too much time looking backward. What is done is done. Raging against the unfairness of it will not help, it can only hinder. Look forward. Regard it as a new beginning and as an adventure, which it may well prove to be.

9. Be realistic but not pessimistic. Don't decide to look just for exactly the same sort of job you did before. If your own particular job experience is unique, you are unlikely to find exactly the same again (though you may be lucky and find that another firm has been looking for someone like you for a long time). It is more likely that some aspects of your training will not be used while you will have to develop alternative strengths.

10. You may not be able to realise exactly the same salary and package of incentives. Don't waste time and energy in regrets. Concentrate on the positive aspects of your new position.

When Jeffrey first heard talk of voluntary redundancy in the oil company for which he worked, he realised it was prudent to take a long, hard look at his lifestyle and to consider very seriously what he would really like to do next.

He had always been deeply involved in his work, though fortunately, he never felt that work was the only love of his life. He even felt that he would like to stop before retirement age. So he was receptive to the thought that he might go on to do something quite different.

His first decision was not to offer for voluntary redundancy, but to wait until he was specifically asked, so that he was in a position to negotiate better terms.

Secondly, he made the decision to move out of the oil business, and when he was offered part-time work in the same field, he declined. Because he had a good job in a progressive firm he was offered a reasonable pension and a golden handshake. Such details are obviously essential considerations if you want to even begin to manage on the money you have behind you.

Both Jeffrey and his wife, Angela, didn't want to go on living in commuter land. Their prosperous Surrey home town had less charm for them than before, mainly because they felt the materialistic values that were all-important there didn't match up to their own beliefs.

Where to live next didn't present a great problem, because over the years they had got to know a Norfolk village near the Broads. Some long-standing friends had taken the decision to move up there permanently a year earlier, so the fact that they would know at least one other couple certainly helped the decision, although it was not the sole reason for moving there.

Cashing in their house and moving to a pleasant but smaller cottage in a less expensive area meant that the couple had an extra injection of money to put towards their future income. With the golden handshake and the pension, it was enough to live on if they were prudent, and did not involve any penny-pinching.

So evolved the decision as to what Jeffrey would do next. He would realise a boyhood dream and build his own boat.

Up in Norfolk, he rented space in a local boatyard and got used to feeling so cold that his hands wouldn't operate until halfway through the morning. He bought a fibreglass hull of a Norfolk Broads yacht and set about building a three berther.

Although time didn't press, Jeffrey worked an 8.30am to 5.30pm day for nearly a year to build his boat. Over the months he found helpful local people who took an interest in his project and gave advice and assistance when he needed it. The discipline of time-keeping helped, Jeffrey feels sure, to ease the break between full-time employment and his new lifestyle.

By the time his boat was finished, he and Angela were well integrated into village life. Even so, although neither of them particularly likes gardening, they joined the local horticultural club purely to meet local people.

The result, five years later, is that they are both very happy in their new life. It was Angela who had more of a problem settling down, partly because of family problems she had to cope with long distance. Her great interest is singing in a choir, but she has found difficulty in joining a local choir that sings the type of music she prefers.

Now the boat is finished, Jeffrey is turning his attention to improving his cottage – making a flint-stone wall was one challenge, and soon he will start to renovate the kitchen. What then?

All this time he has maintained another interest, that of buying and selling antique books, and he is looking to this interest to provide his next paying hobby.

When Pat, at 40 years old, was made redundant for the second time, she sat down and wrote a list of all the things she really enjoyed doing, then gradually allied those enjoyments to her particular skills – organising, getting on well with people etc. Gradually she came up with an idea of providing off-beat country walking holidays.

Whilst recognising that her academic skills were

rather light on the ground, she was a gregarious well-travelled woman who knew what discerning holiday-makers required, and set out to provide it for them.

WHO ARE YOU?

Regardless of its outcome, being made redundant or any form of enforced change of lifestyle encourages us to look deeply at who we really are.

It is a good thing to take stock from time to time of where we are going in life and the sort of people we have become. When such revelations are forced upon us it can be a devastating experience, but nevertheless enriching.

In the busy hubbub of getting on with day-to-day matters, the times for self-reflection are limited, especially when you combine a pressured job with family commitments.

Very often in the process of earning a living, keeping up with the Joneses, maintaining the family intact and reasonably happy, you submerge your own preferences and inclinations in order to do what is best for others. It can come as quite a shock to realise that it is many years since you sat down and played the piano (the previous love of your life) or went dancing or off for a weekend walking or attended church regularly.

Similarly you will almost certainly regard yourself as a sensitive, caring person, mindful of others less fortunate, a friend in need etc. But is this really you or are you always too busy to listen to friends in distress or too cynical to help raise funds for the third world?

CHANGE IN STATUS

All those who have held down jobs will recognise that they are known by job titles. As soon as we enter the workforce, usually at an early age, we are labelled.

'What do you do?' is a question it seems we will answer ten million times in the years ahead. We wear our job titles like protective clothing. As long as we can cling to one we are assured of some kind of status. According to our ambitions, we seek to increase that status. No visible sign of our success is as sought after as a title that shows we have arrived.

If we are at the beginning of our careers, the explanation of a job title is often supported by, 'but I'm studying to be . . .' or, 'I'm hoping to be a . . .' Many women at home bringing up their children explain away domesticity with, 'I'm at home just now but I shall be going back to . . . when the children start school'.

What happens when we are made redundant or retire? The job title vanishes and we are left in limbo. Whether we have been a part-time shop assistant or a managing director, to be bereft of this prop leaves us feeling high and dry.

It can be highly disturbing for a man to be deprived of his title, but his wife will find that she too has lost status and her particular role. It may be in the particular area of business functions they both used to attend. The business 'friends' may vanish or you may find that you are discreetly put 'on ice' for a while to enable you to regain your status or disappear for ever over the distant horizon.

Widows, recently bereaved, often feel this acutely. They are left seeming almost invisible while the outside world adjusts to their new position.

The emphasis on status also changes much closer to home. It will be reflected in your relationships with your family – not just your husband or wife but also with your children. Very often they will assume, at least at first, a protective role. Their unspoken message may be, 'You've had enough to cope with; we'll shield you from as much as possible as long as we can.' On the other hand, if they have been over-protected themselves, and indulged so that they have never stood on their own feet, they could feel that you have let them down, and they will be more preoccupied with, 'What will happen to me?' than in trying to help you. Yet again, their approach will most likely be a mixture of all three. It will vary according to their moods and your own, as well as how well things turn out, as you tackle difficulties that arise and rely on your own internal resources of strength.

You may think that these attitudes will only appear if the change has been sudden, but this is not so. Any person in work knows that, sooner or later, given good health to carry on, they will reach retirement age, but often they act as if it is something that only happens to other people.

If you acknowledge that this lack of title is going to hit you and affect the attitude of those around you, what can be done? The most positive attitude is to recognise that it will happen and when it does you must be prepared to meet it. Think about it in detail and look for areas in which you can compensate. Status in hobby interests can help enormously and so can positions of trust in the local community. It may be time to take up voluntary work, join a society or take a more active role in the church. Part-time work, if you can find it, may provide an answer, as may setting up a business of your own.

It takes time to adjust to any change, but this particular one may take longer than you think, partly because it is so seldom recognised or brought out into the open.

RETIREMENT

Once you are not flat out week after week earning a living, the empty space suddenly available to you may seem unnerving. However well you have planned what to do, that first day of the rest of your life will seem a little strange.

It's not a bad idea to take a few days off if the more pressing need of looking for some kind of work is not your problem. Think about a mini-holiday, a few days away from home so that you can come back fresh to your future lifestyle. If that isn't practical, what about a really good day out to somewhere you have never visited before?

Ideally, your future leisure time should be divided – in what proportions depends on you – between some kind of work, whether paid or voluntary, exercise, hobbies and some activity that stretches your mind in a different way from what would be needed in the other three. If your hobbies are practical, consider taking up bridge or chess or joining a computer course. If they are academic what about car maintenance or woodwork?

Exercise is discussed more fully in Chapter 6, Good Health, but some of these activities, if not all of them, should involve mixing with people – and with as wide an age range as you can find. It is all too easy to find your horizons narrowing without realising it. If you watch current affairs programmes on television and read the newspapers regularly, you may feel that you are in tune with the great wide world, but unless you actually rub shoulders with people and are exposed to their ideas and thoughts, it is easier than you may realise to develop a narrower view of life. By being constantly exposed to new things – both good and bad – you can keep your mind agile, or you could find that you develop a 'them and us' silent war with the rest of the world. The 'Colonel Blimp' and 'Disgusted of Tunbridge Wells' both started out as ordinary folk like everyone else, but because they were never questioned or forced to rethink their views, they gradually became more and more extreme.

Have you ever noticed how people who are never challenged get more and more pompous and in love with the sound of their own voices? Although it may be uncomfortable at times, there is nothing like a family or close friend who can cut us down to size or give kindly ridicule when we need it, to keep us in touch with reality and stop us regarding ourselves as the fount of all wisdom.

Losing the set routine of going to an office every day, or conversely, seeing your other half disappear regularly leaving you to do your own thing at home, can prove a tricky problem to tackle.

Women whose husbands retire very often complain that they can't get on and do things now that he is home, nor can they take off and visit friends or spend a day shopping without feeling guilty or rushing back to get a meal.

If wives are still working and go out leaving their men at home, it can prove even more difficult, especially if the husband happens to believe a wife's place is at his side. If the woman is younger, the last thing she may want to do is give up the job which keeps her at least in pocket money and gives much needed companionship.

Such matters are not easily resolved. It is no good thinking that you can ignore it and the problem will disappear. It needs tact and a good deal of open discussion before it can be resolved.

Many men are ill-equipped for retirement and have no clear idea of what they will do all day to fill the space between getting up from the breakfast table and settling down to watch television after tea. Women are more used to filling their day with hobbies, housework and visiting friends.

Even if you are prepared for retirement, it will take a while to settle down in to some kind of regular pattern. Don't worry too much if it is thoroughly unsettling for a while. Get used to doing at least some things on your own – whether husband or wife. Don't become Siamese twins in your efforts to fill the day. There is nothing more irritating to a wife than a husband who comes shopping because he is bored and then spends time buying what they don't really need or chivvying her to hurry back home.

By all means go on outings together; the pleasure of extra leisure time is what retirement should be about, but maintain your own separate interests and hobbies so that you always have something to discuss and can retain your own separate identities.

CHANGE THROUGH ILLNESS

One of the most traumatic areas of change that one is likely to encounter is a major change of lifestyle due to serious illness. Whether it is our own or that of a partner, it can be frightening and give rise to considerable uncertainty.

Apart from bringing home the fact that we are not immortal, we may have to accept that our earning capacity may be severely curtailed, or even cease, and that we will have to rearrange the way we go about life.

Victims of heart-related diseases will find that they must take life more slowly and try much harder than before to avoid stress. Arthritis victims will experience curtailed activity. Each major illness has its limitations, but now, thanks to medical advances, the forecasts for recovery are better than ever before.

Apart from the support offered by hospitals, GPs and health visitors, there is an additional back-up of the associations and support groups that offer valuable advice and assistance from people who have experienced similar difficulties to those you are now facing. It is particularly helpful to contact such a society if you are caring for someone and feel high and dry in terms of practical advice and information.

Your first preoccupation if illness strikes is survival, but after the immediate fight is over there will be long periods of frustration and depression. You will feel that you are making little progress and that to keep on making the effort is just too much. This is just the time when a positive, optimistic approach is vital. So much can be accomplished if you can establish the will and determination to improve. If it is your partner who is ill, you will also have to have hope and confidence, and on some days, enough for both of you.

Apart from accepting all the help on offer from your GP and hospital adviser, you can contact the social services for aids that may make life easier. If you need walking-frames or similar items of equipment, ask for them, or if they are not available via that avenue, contact your local Red Cross office to see if you can get them that way. Talk to anyone who has had a similar illness and find out all you can through books etc.

It will take months, sometimes even years, to really come to terms with the enforced change, largely of course, depending on the degree of debility. Don't ever feel that you can't improve. Sometimes comparatively trivial medical complaints can loom large on your list of difficulties, but if you mention them, you may find that there is a simple remedy available.

If you are looking after someone who is recovering from severe illness, it is important to go on treating him or her normally, as before. Don't talk in front of him as if he isn't there or cannot hear what is being said. If there are temporary speech defects, don't answer questions on his behalf if it is just a question of giving him time to answer them himself. Avoid finishing off sentences. It is even true to say that you shouldn't be too protective in your approach, as unless considerable effort is made on all sides, progress will be nil or very slow.

Tackling the practical problems that arise will ease your mind and keep you busy instead of spending too much time worrying. Make sure you are getting all benefits such as sick pay, supplementary benefit, if appropriate, mobility allowance, invalidity benefit, attendance allowance, if any of these apply to you. All these allowances have strict guidelines, and it can take some effort and determination to find out those to which you are entitled. Don't necessarily give up if you are told you cannot have one allowance if you feel you are entitled to it. You can always appeal, or contact your doctor or the association that specialises in your particular disability for their advice on whether you should press your claim. Enquire about whether you are entitled to a home help or whether Meals on Wheels would be appropriate. You may be entitled to an early pension from the employer or you may have contributed to an insurance policy that will now pay up.

It may be an appropriate time to see how you can make your home easier to run. Could you plan to have electric sockets higher up the wall instead of on the skirting-board? Pull-cord switches for lights make life easier. You may need to change your seating – for example, a higher chair that makes it easier to get up and down. Can you indulge in an infra-red remote control television that you can operate from your chair?

You can get advice and ideas for home-made aids, as well as those to be purchased, if you write to the *Royal Association for Disability and Rehabilitation (RADAR)* or the *Disabled Living Foundation* (see Address List below).

Address List

Action on Phobias, 17 Burlington Place, Eastbourne, E. Sussex BN21 4AR. 0323 54755

Asthma Research Council, 300 Upper Street, London N1 2XX. 01 226 2260

British Diabetic Association, 10 Queen Anne Street, London W1M 0BD. 01 323 1531

British Heart Foundation, 102 Gloucester Place, London W1H 4DH. 01 935 0185

British Red Cross Society, 9 Grosvenor Crescent, London SW1X 7EJ. 01 235 5454

British Rheumatism and Arthritis Association, 6 Grosvenor Crescent, London SW1X 7ER. 01 235 0902

Chest, Heart and Stroke Association, Tavistock House North, Tavistock Square, London WC1H 9JE. 01 387 3012

Citizens' Advice Bureau, see local telephone directory or National Association of Citizens' Advice Bureaux below

Disabled Advice Centre, Atheldene Community Centre, Garratt Lane, London SW18 4DU. 01 870 7437

Disabled Living Foundation, 380 Harold Road, London W9 2HU. 01 289 6111

Multiple Sclerosis Society, 25 Effie Road, London SW6 1EE. 01 736 6267

National Association of Citizens' Advice Bureaux, 115–123 Pentonville Road, London N1 9LZ. 01 833 2181

Parkinson's Disease Society, 36 Portland Place, London W1N 3DG. 01 323 1174

Pensioner's Link, 17 Balfe Street, London N1 9EB. 01 278 5501

Phobics Society, 4 Cheltenham Road, Chorlton-cum-Hardy, Manchester M21 1QN.

Royal Association for Disability and Rehabilitation (RADAR), 25 Mortimer Street, London W1N 8AB. 01 637 5400

Royal National Institute for the Blind, 224 Great Portland Street, London W1N 6AA. 01 388 1266

Royal National Institute for the Deaf, 105 Gower Street, London WC1 E 6AH. 01 387 8033

2

WAYS TO WORK

Many people are finding that it is still possible to obtain paid work after retirement or after redundancy in later years. True, it may be quite different from your previous employment and the remuneration may not be the same, but there are still opportunities around in many parts of the country, if you can go out and find them.

What often happens is that your old friends network will rally round and put you in touch with someone who is looking for a person with your sort of experience. Sometimes those in similar jobs to yours in other firms, people you may have known during working days, will pass on your name.

If you have worked in a profession, you may be retained as a consultant on a part-time basis, or you may be invited to join a smaller company who could not have afforded someone of your experience and expertise when you were at the peak of your career.

You may find an employment agency in your area that specialises in placing more mature people in jobs.

Some people become self-employed and act as consultants in their previous line of business, or take the plunge and do something completely different. Setting up your own small business, even a one-man business can work if you have a particular skill that others will pay for. It may be a hobby you have developed over the years or it may be knowledge you gained in your job. It could be that you have a flair for organising others that can be put to good use. Your first port of call should be your own manager or personnel department, if there is one, who should be able to advise you on what is available within the firm. If your redundancy is because of rationalisation, or trimming the workforce to save overheads, they may be willing to employ you on a freelance basis. This is more common in some industries than others, but it could mean that you are offered a redundancy package and then have the chance to take back at least part of your job as a self-employed person.

Although at face value this may seem the best of all possible worlds, it does, of course, have its pitfalls. The job may not last very long, you may be offered poor terms to do the job as a freelance and you will have very little protection if anything goes wrong. You will probably have to set up your own office at home, pay out for typewriters, secretarial help and filing systems as well as pay your own overheads like telephone, travelling etc.

The plus points are that it gives you a base salary while you try to make a go of self-employment and find other clients. You can make your own decisions and work in a more flexible way.

Even if such an offer is not on the table, your manager may know of other firms in the area who will be looking for workers.

CAREER ADVICE

This may be a time to approach a firm of career consultants who can advise you on the right course to adopt, although they are unlikely to find you work. What they can do is analyse your skills and identify your personality sufficiently accurately to show you what path you could take.

They can discover, for instance, whether you have the necessary skills and personality to become successfully self-employed, whether you have sufficient drive and initiative to work on your own, whether you can lead a team, whether you are best with things or people. Although you may think that in maturity you know yourself pretty well, it helps to have someone else identify these traits independently and to discuss them dispassionately.

31

A common procedure is to fill in a very detailed questionnaire before attending for a day of aptitude tests and a one-to-one counselling session. Most analysts will take people up to 55 years of age, but after that, as the chances of retraining for a career are obviously lessened, they would arrange a consultation first. Fees vary, but as a day spent there could change the rest of your life – to advantage – it could be money well spent.

What the analysts don't do is find you a job, but they do aim to point you in the right direction, and they should help you to prepare a curriculum vitae and present yourself well at an interview.

Sometimes they may suggest a period of retraining. People in their early forties, for example, could afford to retrain for two years and still have anything up to twenty years of work experience ahead. This is something that is often overlooked when trying to decide what to do for the rest of your life. Twenty years is a long time by anyone's standards, so don't dismiss retraining without serious consideration (see Chapter 3, A Chance to Learn).

Norma was 34 and had been at home with her children for some years when she decided the time was right to take her future more seriously.

Before she left work she had held various minor secretarial posts, and now felt that much as she would like to return to work, there should be something more challenging that she could do.

She consulted *Career Analysts*, and tests revealed that although she had only four O-levels, she had a much higher intellectual rating than that implied. She was stable, sensitive and independently minded. Added to which, she had good verbal skills, was logical and had the desire to be of service to people.

Her counsellor suggested that she should consider a career in law and study to be a solicitor. This meant several years of study and a further period of being articled in a solicitor's office. Nevertheless, by the time she was 40 she would be in a rewarding career with a good twenty years ahead of her in which to practise.

After a great deal of thought and discussion with her family, Norma took the advice and has now just qualified in what promises to be satisfying work.

SUCCESS AFTER SIXTY AGENCY

One or two employment agencies now exist especially for older workers. *Success after Sixty* is probably one of the better known, although they will find work for people of 55 and above. They operate mainly from London, but also have a branch in Croydon, Surrey.

Most of their clients are smaller firms who cannot undertake training themselves, and so welcome the chance to take on people with experience. The jobs available are normally office ones. Temporary work is quite often on offer and this is encouraged as it gives both the company and the employee a chance to get to know each other before taking on too much of a commitment.

Stanley was an early-retired chartered secretary who approached them for a job. After one or two unsuccessful interviews for book-keeping positions, he was offered a more specialised one/two day a week job with a firm of solicitors as a capital gains tax clerk. Four years later he is still happy in the job which he shares with a gent approaching 80.

Monica spends two days a week as book-keeper to a husband and wife team of antique dealers, coping with their accounts and VAT. She has been with them now for several years and regards herself as a member of the family.

PART-TIME OPPORTUNITIES

Part-time work is very often preferred by older people, and it seems that jobs are a little easier to find. *PartTime Careers* is London based and finds that they can usually place people up to around 60 years of age. All their jobs are office-based and include accountants, receptionists, book-keepers and secretaries. They try to match people who want four mornings or two afternoons a week with firms looking for a similar commitment. All their situations are based in the West End or City of London, although there are occasionally some in the inner suburbs.

Part-time work will rarely be combined with any on-the-job training. Indeed you may be thrown in at the deep end and hardly introduced to colleagues. Traditionally, part-time workers were rather looked down upon by permanent staff and given the worst office equipment and the draughty seat by the door. This is gradually changing now that office work is getting easier to come by on a part-time basis, as there are several advantages to employers. The main benefit to employers is that they can often fit the necessary work into a few days a week and cut down on basic costs of paying staff for time not used.

Part-timers are protected by employment legislation only if they work more than eight hours per week. For those working eight to sixteen hours, five years service is required instead of the usual two years. There are proposals to make the bottom limit twelve hours.

Some part-time work will be offered to you as a permanent job with a contract of employment and for some you may be expected to act as self-employed and pay your own tax and national insurance. The benefits of being on the permanent staff may include receiving proportionate sick pay and holiday entitlement, but it is not automatic and you are unlikely to be included in a pension scheme.

The problem of what to do about all the bank holidays if you happen to work every Monday has to be resolved between you and the employer. Some are philosophical and pay you regardless, but others expect you to work an alternative day instead.

If you work part time as a self-employed person, you cannot expect to be paid if you don't attend. This means that when you take a holiday or are off sick you are earning nothing, so bear this in mind when considering the overall pay offered between one job and another.

Work in shops, restaurants and pubs has always been

available and still is in many parts of the country. Pay is usually low, though it can sometimes be supplemented by tips from customers. The hours may be unsocial but they are also extremely flexible, and you can usually find something to fit in with your particular lifestyle. In addition evening or night work can sometimes be found in residential homes for the elderly if you are of a caring disposition and reasonably active.

ARMED FORCES

Anyone from the non-commissioned ranks of the armed forces can approach the *Regular Forces Employment Association* which has been in existence for over 100 years. Anyone who has served three years or more and has a good character reference is eligible. Most of the candidates have served periods of between three and twelve years although some have been in the services for the full 22 years. The Association expects to deal with around 11,500 people in a year of which they will be able to help around 43 per cent. They cover any field of employment.

A similar service exists for commissioned ranks from the *Officers' Association*.

THE PROFESSIONS

If you are a member of a professional association it is worthwhile making enquiries to see if they have details of any work available. Very often people who need someone with a particular skill may approach the association for recommendations and they may operate a jobs register.

In some cases you may find the salary is less than you might have been used to. You may decide that you would rather do other things, but if you are looking for a top-up to a pension or a way to continue an interest in your profession it may fulfil these criteria.

Many recruitment agencies specialise in particular kinds of work such as accountancy, book-keeping, nursing, medical health care, social work. If you belong to a union they may have a register of vacancies, so make enquiries.

PART-TIME WORK

It pays to consider part-time work if, for example, you are trying to start up your own business and realise that it is not, as yet, a full-time occupation. If you have family commitments, they can often be fitted in as hours can be quite flexible. It is also a chance to get to know an industry better to see whether you like it – and an opportunity to get more involved than you would by just taking a temporary position for a couple of weeks or so. It can also keep you financially afloat if you are retraining (see Chapter 3, A Chance to Learn).

PERSONAL CONTACTS

Personal contacts are still the best route to finding new jobs. This doesn't mean to say you should ring up friend Peter and ask him for a job. The chances are you will lose a friend as well as not find the job. What you can do is ask him to let you know if he hears of any jobs that might be suitable, or by mentioning your name if anyone asks him. He might also be able to give you a lead if anyone is leaving a position that might fit, and he could suggest you write to other contacts of his who might be in a position to help.

Remember that however friendly you may be, he will probably not know a great deal about the sort of job you held down or even what experience you have. To be of real value, your friend should have your curriculum vitae so that if he is in a position to pass on your name to someone else, it is as a specific candidate not just the name of a mate who could do with some assistance.

Business acquaintances should be approached discreetly but in a similar way. Beware of the professional jealousies which beset any industry, and choose your confidants with care.

Where possible, it is better to suggest an informal meeting rather than transfix anyone on the phone. Some people don't respond well to telephone calls, and in any case you cannot know whether you have telephoned at a sensible time.

If you have any high-level contacts, such as managing directors or chairmen of companies that you have dealt with and who know you fairly well, it is worthwhile sending them an informal note to say that you are now on the job market and could they spare a few minutes to give you any advice on the climate for jobs and the industry in general. If they respond, all well and good, their time and advice will be invaluable. If not, you won't have lost anything.

Whether or not any of this casting of bread upon the waters comes to anything, it is courteous and always appreciated if you drop them all a note of thanks for their time.

Avoid communicating with them too often from then on – even those anxious to help will tire of endless phone calls. Make a note of what each person said he or she might be able to do, if anything, and make contact again three or four weeks later. Even better, when you are parting company after your initial chat, set your own time scale for the next contact. It's easier to say at that point, 'I'll ring/contact you again in two or three weeks if I may,' so that your call can be expected or anticipated.

One strange thing about looking for a job, especially after redundancy, is that leads often come from those least expected to help. Your close colleagues or immediate superiors often sympathise or express support but do little about it. Very often it is people on the fringe or those you feel you hardly know who turn up trumps.

WORKING FOR YOURSELF

A significant number of men and women seriously consider going it alone at one time or another, and the numbers of those who put it into action is increasing annually.

Normally it will start as pocket-money work – not enough to earn a living but a very useful extra. Most folk can make some money from something they can do at home, but far fewer can earn the equivalent of their previous salary – at least not at first.

Deciding what to do is probably not as important as knowing whether you have the right temperament. You may love or hate the idea of doing everything yourself – from phoning customers, buying the stamps and coping with advertising.

You may have spent your life in the environment of being supervised either closely or loosely, and to find there is no-one looking over your shoulder has an adverse effect on your determination and stickability.

You will need to make your own decisions about everything from whether you need more envelopes to taking on a helper should your business expand. Being in business on your own is a lonely occupation. How will you face up to that, bearing in mind that most people go out to work for company as well as for money?

Are you well organised? You could have the most brilliant business idea of the decade, but unless you can follow it through and cope with all the administration and paperwork it will be stillborn. You need good health and the ability to work long hours to get your project off the ground. How will your family feel if you are working at weekends instead of going out and about with them? How do you cope when you feel depressed? Are you the kind who can grit your teeth and get on with the job in hand or do you sink into despondency and take days to recover? You will need to be able to bounce back when things go wrong, and not spend the rest of your life feeling a failure when you meet setbacks.

Those are the questions you should ask yourself before you even think about taking it a stage further – finding something to do. Think deeply and consider asking a close friend or someone in your family you know will give you a reasoned answer whether they think you have such qualities.

Being self-employed is tough and it will certainly make you harder and more self-reliant. You will learn to make your own decisions – for better or worse – and enjoy the process. It may change your personality, so be prepared for your family to notice the difference.

What can you do? must be the second question to answer. Your most obvious first port of call will be an extension of what you have been doing in paid employment, especially if it is an obvious service skill such as book-keeping, nursing, hair-dressing or teaching. Professional skills such as these are generally in demand, and even more so these days are technical skills such as carpentry, plumbing, painting and decorating.

Other services in demand will be gardening or window-cleaning if you live in an area where people can afford such luxuries. Domestic cleaning is another.

You may think of a comparatively little-known service that would be welcome in your area. It might be something you wished was on offer while you were at work or something your friends have discussed from time to time.

> Lindy set up a home-search agency in the area where she lived, to help people house hunting at a distance to find exactly what they wanted without having to spend fruitless weekends racing up and down the motorway.

> Jan offered to match people's china to replace broken cups and saucers by setting up a register of owners willing to part with specific pieces.

If such service areas are not for you, do you have a hobby that could be made to pay? Pottery, calligraphy, basketry, genealogy, beadwork, knitting, philately may all be earners if you approach matters in the right way.

If you lack the confidence to feel you could earn money this way, you may find that you can improve your technique by taking a government training scheme or an evening class. There may be a guild of fellow enthusiasts in your area (see Chapter 3, A Chance to Learn). An alternative morale booster is to visit shops that sell the sort of goods you are interested in, and study the standard and general finish of each article. Most people are reassured when they see what is already on the market and the general standard of quality – reassured because they know they could do better. Indeed it is this very fact that has stimulated some to get going. (See Dick's story on page 11). You will soon get the feel of whether your work is of a sufficiently high standard to sell to the public.

Once you have decided what line your business will take, there comes the long and painstaking task of assessing the market. Will anyone want the service or the goods you have to offer? Are there many competitors in the field, and how good are they? What do they charge? You must take time to research this side of things very thoroughly.

You also need to know who your customers will be. If you plan to offer the kind of service that is only required by wealthy people, are there enough of them in your area? Do you prefer to make a few expensive goods for the exclusive few or would you rather concentrate on the masses?

Take advantage of all the advice on offer from professional people as well as those in similar businesses. Professional advice is, of course, valuable in assessing whether your scheme is viable, whether you have thought sufficiently about cash flow, the amount of time it takes to build up a business before it makes you any money, and whether you have assessed the market accurately. What they won't know, apart from sizing you up at consultations, is whether you have the temperament and discipline.

On the other hand, your friends and family will know only too well what sort of person you are, but have probably little idea about the business side, so their views could be illuminating and useful too. The government is actively encouraging the starting up of small businesses and it is possible to go on one of their various courses (see page 58). These are extremely valuable and you will get first class personal advice.

The *Small Firms Service*, also run by the government, is a network of advice centres throughout the country where counselling is available. Sometimes simple queries can be answered over the phone. The counsellors are all experienced businessmen who know the pitfalls and difficulties you are likely to encounter. They can help you with all sorts of queries, from how to approach your bank manager for a loan to finding out about any planning permission you may need.

Any discussion with them is confidential and initial advice is free. If you want further sessions, after your initial one, a small charge is made. If you want to talk to a special consultant or adviser, they can introduce you to experts but they will make their normal professional charges. To contact your nearest *Small Firms Service* dial 100 and ask for Freefone Enterprise.

For small businesses in rural areas you can contact the *Council For Small Industries in Rural Areas (COSIRA)*. Their aim is to get small businesses started in rural areas and they offer an information service and consultancy. They can also provide training and run weekend business seminars. They may be able to offer grants or loans. Look for them in your local telephone directory or write to the head office.

Another initiative aimed to encourage people to set up their own business is the Enterprise Allowance Scheme. This is to help those who have been unemployed for at least eight weeks and you must be receiving either unemployment or supplementary benefit when you apply.

If you can show that you have at least £1000 that you are willing to invest in your business over the first twelve months, you may be eligible for an allowance of £40 a week for up to 52 weeks.

There are other conditions that must be met; for example, that your proposed business must be approved by the *Manpower Services Commision* and you should be under pensionable age.

To find out more ask at your local Jobcentre or *Small Firms Service*. Many areas these days have their own Enterprise Agencies and these are interested in helping those who wish to start up a small business that is likely to employ others rather than a one-man business. Sometimes you can get help in the terms of loans or grants and cheap rents for business premises. Ask the *Small Firms Service* if there is an agency in your area or write to *Business in the Community*. Your local council may have a scheme, so it is always worth making enquiries.

There are many who find considerable fulfilment in meeting the challenges that running their own business will bring. Very often they don't even set out in that direction.

Eleanor was in her late forties when she gave up her job and moved to the country with her husband. For the first year she was quite happy doing up the house and getting to know the area, but after that, time started to hang heavily and she looked around for something to do.

She had always been interested in crafts, and started to make herbal pillows, pot-pourri cushions and matching kitchen aprons and oven gloves.

By selling at craft fairs, she soon discovered what sold well and what was less popular. She also found she preferred the designing and selling to the physical task of making up the goods.

Eleanor found two local outworkers and set them to making the items while she designed and then sold the work. One interesting way she found to sell stock was to talk to women's groups about the history of herbs, including pot-pourri, and then offer items for sale at the end of question time.

Because most of the meetings were in the evening, it gave her time during the day to organise and sell to shops. By visiting local towns, she found five or six stockists who took her work on a regular basis, which she found was more rewarding financially than going to London in the hope of interesting the busy buyers of department stores.

For the first few years Eleanor worked from home, but found all the materials and readymade items took up more and more space. She decided to move operations to a local craft centre where she could attend at busy times such as weekends and public holidays, yet when she needed to be away from the site, there was someone else to look after her shop.

Eleanor is hoping to expand her operation and take on more outworkers, and is considering appointing agents to represent her in selling to shops. In this way she will have the extra time she needs to concentrate on designing and investigating innovations.

James was in his early forties when his engineering job in a remote but beautiful part of south-west England came to an end. There was no hope of getting any similar work unless he was prepared to move right away from the area. Both he and his wife loved where they lived and knew they couldn't bear to leave it.

James' reaction to his problem was to try and make use of one of his hobbies – cooking. He embarked on a short professional cookery course and he intends to take up cooking for private parties with the possibility of running his own catering business in the future.

The other love of his life is music, and he foresees the chance to organise musical soirées along with stylish dinner parties.

James' lifestyle is going to change completely, and his income is almost certainly going to drop, but if you are concerned with the quality of life, as he is, and can make certain readjustments, you may find you can afford to earn considerably less.

One car not two, moving to a less expensive area or trading down your house for a cheaper one, if you are an owner-occupier, can become a not too painful answer to acquiring more cash. This is discussed more fully in Chapter 8, Managing Your Money.

One thing that most of these enthusiasts had in common was accepting the fact that they were no longer nine-to-five people. There is no way you can really get going in a business of your own that will support you, and possibly a family, without being prepared in the early years to make a considerable time commitment. You will be working round the clock and very likely seven days a week.

This of course will involve those around you, so it is important that if you embark on this way of life you have their support. You should not let this time factor (not to mention any financial stringencies) creep up on your partner without discussing it fully first, or you will be heading for trouble. When problems occur, bring them out into the open early on so that any niggles don't spoil the whole project.

Philip was 45 when he was made redundant. Although he had been reasonably successful in his engineering profession, aptitude tests at a career guidance centre amazingly revealed he had no mechanical aptitude. Back in his teens he had chosen his career quite wrongly. He had taken the wrong A-levels and the wrong degree for all the wrong reasons. The only one he could recall after so many years was that he liked being out of doors.

After getting an ordinary degree, he had held down engineering jobs during his early career, but with no great flair. He had a better time when he was moved to management services, where he was concerned with ordering and controlling supplies, budgeting and general efficiency. Once that side of the business became computerised he was struggling again and even resorting to tranquillisers.

His aptitude tests showed that right back at A-level time he should have studied economics and gone on to take accountancy as a qualification.

At 45 it was impractical to consider taking an accountancy exam, but he was advised to look for an administrative job. He was prepared to study the Chartered Secretary syllabus, and it was thought that with his previous managerial experience, an intermediate exam might give him the edge to find suitable work.

Philip decided to follow that advice. He had a cushion of two years' redundancy money along with good personal contacts, and he welcomed the opportunity to find a job with less stress, although consequently less money.

Mollie was made redundant at 54 and decided she didn't want to launch herself into the job market again. By taking early retirement she had a very small pension. In addition she owned her own house and decided she would like to sell up, live in a modest country cottage and invest the extra cash.

Mollie had two major interests, writing and antiques, and she was hoping to supplement her income by developing one or the other. Through assessment, it was seen that she had high literary interests and considerable verbal skills. Further tests showed that she was not a business person, in that she was not likely to be sufficiently tough and assertive when it mattered, and could be taken for a ride. Although she appeared to be willing to take risks, her self-motivation was low.

She was advised to concentrate on her writing and keep the antiques interest as a hobby. Mollie was already halfway through a novel, and her first task would be to finish it and get the advice of a literary agent. In the meantime she could be writing small features and approaching magazines and local papers.

Although she lacked the competitive edge that would give her an entrée into full-time journalism, there appeared to be no reason why she could not supplement her pension in this way.

In contrast, Helen, aged 49, underwent the same tests of personality, intellect and aptitude, and found that basically she was in the right job – freelance journalism. Three years previously she had left her highly paid staff job because of stress and a certain amount of boredom after holding down the same position for many years.

Three years on, she was reasonably satisfied with her life-style, but felt isolated, and was considering opting out of writing and buying a larger house where she could develop a bed and breakfast business.

Tests showed that she had a high degree of verbal skill, was competitive and got on well with people. She lacked persuasive powers and was not very good at selling, including selling herself. In addition she had no entrepreneurial flair and was not particularly aggressive or business minded.

In view of her current success as a freelance writer, it was suggested she should carry on her existing work but look to her social life to provide more outside company. Because her leisure interests, mainly reading, sewing and embroidery, were lone activities, they were increasing the isolation not solving the problem. A group activity – even joining the local amateur dramatic society in any capacity – would use her interests and get her involved with people.

CASUAL WORK

Casual work has added advantages besides earning useful cash. It can give you a chance to learn new skills and meet different people.

Much of the work is rather boring, but it does give you useful experience that may help when you find a permanent job.

A lot of casual work is of the opportunist variety, in that you have to be prepared to act immediately it becomes available, or offer yourself before the job is even advertised. You may see a need yourself and offer to help out. If you see a job on offer, it won't do to go home and think about it or plan your letter of application. You will need to move quickly there and then.

What is available may depend very largely on service skills. It may be work in pubs, hotels or restaurants where you can work as kitchen or bar staff, at waiting or cleaning.

There may be seasonal work in shops, at sales time or at Christmas, for instance. In the country you may be able to pick fruit or vegetables. During the summer you may be able to get outdoor work as a jobbing gardener, either in private houses or from the local park or garden centre.

Market stalls or car boot sales can provide interesting openings. Car boot sales are informal affairs where you can pay for your pitch beforehand or pay slightly more on the day. You can normally sell anything, so all your dusty treasures at the back of the cupboard can be turned to profit. You can beg discarded objects from friends or you can sell your own home-produced crafts. Once you sell food you are bound by regulations regarding health and hygiene. Ask your local Environmental Health Officer.

An alternative, if cooking really interests you, might be to contribute to one of the many excellent Women's Institute markets up and down the country. The bonus here is that, if accepted as a regular contributor, they will advise you on what to cook, how to package and label it to meet health requirements and also how to price it. It is a wonderful way to start off, and although you won't make your fortune, it is one of the pleasanter ways of finding out whether you will enjoy the work and making the same thing week after week. Contact the local

Market Controller or send a stamped self-addressed envelope for more details to the Market Adviser at the *Federation of Women's Institutes*. To rent a stall in a local market, you may have to apply to the local council, if they run it, or to the particular market's organiser. Not all welcome casual stallholders, and you may have to rent it for a set period, but it is worth enquiring. Some private markets operate just at the weekend and welcome casual stallholders.

One enterprising woman started in a private market selling part of her extensive fashion wardrobe. She borrowed a dress rail, hired a trestle table and went armed with a garden chair and flask of coffee. She sold 50 per cent of her stock on the first day and could have sold more had her clothes been a larger size. After that she sold clothes that friends had discarded for a small commission. Although she had no intention of making it a career, it gave her some useful pocket money and a highly entertaining day out.

Pat worked for one of the major service industries in the customer services department. At 47 she knew she couldn't spend the years to her retirement working with her existing colleagues – their attitude drove her mad.

She had few qualifications, but a bright, outgoing personality that made her popular with people. She was confident, independent minded and prepared to take risks.

After a lot of thought, and a fair amount of practice at car boot sales, she and a friend took on a market stall selling cane work, and it appears to be going well. She loves the cut and thrust of market life and is gradually getting resigned to the number of times it can rain. Her turnover is improving and she is looking for ways to expand the business.

How to find Casual Work

Look for advertisements in the newsagent's window, the local pub, restaurant or in the office/shop window.

Make a direct approach to anyone who may want helpers: the personnel department in a large store or the manager of a shop or garden centre. Some of the larger firms may advertise in the local paper. Word of mouth is still an effective way of finding a likely source of work – some places take on helpers year after year and the local people will know when to look out.

It may pay you to draft your own advert to put in a shop window presenting your skills in the best possible light.

OTHER WORK

Minicab driving work may be available, although the hours are unsocial, but that applies to a lot of casual work. You will need your own modern four-door car in a good state of repair and a clean licence before you approach any local firms. Then you will need a hire and reward insurance policy. The company that arranges work for you will give you the details.

If you can offer impeccable references, you could look after people's houses and/or pets while they are away. One company that runs such a scheme looks for mature, reliable people who can provide superb references to live in for the period. Demand is highest during conventional holiday times, although some weekend work is available.

It is not a chance to explore new areas whilst living in luxury. You are expected to really look after the house and deter burglars or vandals by being there, so it's no good expecting to be out all day.

You may be asked to feed and exercise pets, tend house plants, take telephone messages etc. For more details look for adverts in glossy magazines or write to *Pet and Property Care Ltd* or *Homesitters*.

OUTWORK

Unskilled work done in your own home for a manufacturer is usually classed as outwork or homework. It will also include other jobs such as addressing envelopes. It may be assembly work such as putting together Christmas crackers or packets of table napkins. It could be work in the fashion industry such as stitching skirts.

You will almost certainly be paid by the item, which is known as piece-work or piece-rate, rather than by time spent. It is nearly always badly paid.

The secret, if you undertake this type of work, is to get organised and build yourself up to an ordered assembly line so that you can achieve a steady rate. In the beginning you will almost certainly be slow and clumsy and make virtually nothing.

Some industries – such as toy and women's clothing manufacturers – are covered by wages councils who establish a minimum rate for the job, but there is no protection against the work drying up, and no holiday pay or sickness benefit. If you are offered work, you can check with the *Citizens' Advice Bureau* about whether you are covered. Some jobs offered to homeworkers may include storing flammable materials or strong-smelling glues at home, so be aware that it may cause a fire risk and check you are covered within your home insurance policy. Even if there is no fire risk, you can sometimes find that what you are asked to assemble is bulky and it takes over your living-room before you know where you are.

The best way to find this type of work is to ask amongst your friends and see if they work for a company and whether they are reasonably satisfied with their payment and conditions.

Some small business people – possibly working from home themselves – may need outworkers to do some of the basic tasks. Where they are taking on only one or two people, they are more likely to look after reliable people who are meticulous and deliver the goods on time.

If you are offered work, don't sign anything unless you really understand it. A manufacturer may put in a clause enabling him to refuse any batch of work with a single mistake in it, meaning you could have spent many hours working for nothing. He may even deduct the cost of the materials. If you reply to advertisements in newspapers or magazines, don't send any money, and beware of the advert that promises you work if you first buy some form of equipment or machinery. While it may be genuine, it could be that once you have made enough items to pay for the machine the work dries up. Be sensible about believing all the promises made about how much you can earn – the higher the sum, the less likely it is to be realistic.

Most employers will want to recruit you on a self-employed basis, so it will be up to you to sort out your own national insurance and income tax.

Outwork is undeniably poorly paid, but on the other hand, if for any reason you are housebound, it is a way of earning a little extra.

ADDRESS LIST

Business in the Community, 227A City Road, London EC1V 1LX. 01 253 3716

Career Analysts, Career House, 90 Gloucester Place, London W1H 9BL. 01 935 5452

Citizens' Advice Bureau, see local telephone directory or see National Association of Citizens' Advice Bureaux below

Council for Small Industries in Rural Areas (COSIRA), Head Office, 141 Castle Street, Salisbury, Wiltshire SP1 3TP. 0722 336255

Federation of Women's Institutes, 39 Eccleston Street, London SW1 9NT. 01 730 7212

Homesitters, Moat Farm, Buckland, Nr. Aylesbury, Bucks HP22 5HY. 0296 631289

Manpower Services Commission, see local telephone directory

National Association of Citizens' Advice Bureaux, 115-123 Pentonville Road, London N1 9LZ. 01 833 2181

Officers' Association, 48 Pall Mall, London SW1Y 5JY. 01 930 0125

Part Time Careers Ltd, 10 Golden Square, London W1R 3AF. 01 437 3103

Pet and Property Care Ltd, 35 Blacklands Road, Benson, Oxon OX9 6NW. 0491 37857

Regular Forces Employment Association, 25 Bloomsbury Square, London WC1A 2LN. 01 637 3918

Small Firms Service, dial 100 and ask for Freefone Enterprise

Success After Sixty (Office Employment) Ltd, 40–41 Old Bond Street, London W1X 3AS. 01 629 9672; and 33 George Street, Croydon, Surrey CRO 1LB. 01 680 0858

3

A CHANCE TO LEARN

The thought of going back to the classroom and becoming a student again after years away from study may be the last thing you have in mind if you find time on your hands. But many people have found it adds a new dimension to their lives, and it has made a profound difference to how they think and view the world outside.

The opportunities to learn are as diverse as the subjects – you don't have to think in terms of a university degree. Learning can be achieved by attending an evening class, a lecture at your local art gallery or museum, a government retraining scheme, or a residential weekend course as well as more committed adult education study or the open university.

By learning at any level, you do more than increase your overall knowledge of the subject. You learn more about yourself in the process, and have the opportunity to mix and meet with people if you attend classes, and even if you embark on self-study courses, there are often summer schools or regular chances to meet other students.

You may wonder why you should bother to strain yourself learning new tricks when you could spend the time pottering around and enjoying hobbies you already know about. Learning enhances much more than you may appreciate.

It gives you greater status when you meet others better educated than yourself. Very many older people, for a variety of reasons, left full-time school with a very sketchy, incomplete education. However well they have 'got on' since then, they themselves know the gaps in their own knowledge. It is a good time to make up what was missed out.

You will get the opportunity to be exposed to new ideas and opinions which may be revelations. You probably won't agree with all of them, but by reasoning out whys and wherefores, you will have made your brain more nimble and you can take the chance to put forward your own views more lucidly and with greater fluency.

If you are prepared to study for some kind of qualification, it may help you get a better job than the one you held previously or to go off and do something quite new.

If you are considering studying seriously – like taking GCSE exams, for example – it may help to take a pre-study course that shows you how to cope. There are techniques in study just as in most things – how to read quickly, take effective notes and write essays. These skills can be learned, and so can exam technique, learning to answer quickly, anticipating likely questions and achieving effective revision.

Although it may sound daunting to have to embark on such a study course before you even begin your subject, it could save you time and a great deal of frustration in the end.

LEISURE CLASSES

If you want to dip your toe in the water, you can attend what can broadly be termed leisure classes – in fact you may have been involved already. These include the hundreds of subjects you can learn at an evening or day class in your local school or college or community centre. Your total involvement here is a couple of hours a week, with possibly some extra study required in between.

Courses are most often run by the local education authority but voluntary groups get involved and the *Workers' Educational Association (WEA)* may run courses in your area.

Many start in the autumn and run for a set number of weeks, sometimes just for the length of a school term and sometimes for seven or eight months.

They can lead to passing exams, and each will be explained in the syllabus. Booklets or descriptive leaflets list each class available and give you a pretty good indication of the level of study that will be involved. Read the class descriptions carefully. Details are usually widely available around August at your local library or at the schools themselves. Fees vary, you may get them reduced if you are of pensionable age or unemployed. Conditions vary according to region, so do ask.

Very often the courses are over-subscribed and you are enrolled very much on a first come, first served basis, but if the course you want to take is full up, it may be possible to join up later in the year as people drop out. This can work for some subjects, but less well for others.

Classes can, and usually are discontinued if not enough people attend, so it is in everyone's interest to keep up attendance.

Evening, or part-time day classes are generally enjoyable and a very low-key way of learning. The pace is generally slow but that may suit you, especially to begin with.

RESIDENTIAL COURSES

The tone and pace are normally similar to evening classes. It's a halfway house between an out-and-out holiday and a chance to learn. Classes are usually paced throughout the day. There are sometimes three sessions, morning, afternoon and evening, or sometimes the afternoons or evenings may be free to relax and visit places of interest nearby. The locations can range from beautiful country houses with swimming-pools and croquet lawns to university buildings that are empty while the students are on vacation. Others are commercial ventures run by enterprising hotel groups.

Fees vary considerably and so does the standard of accommodation and catering. It is a most agreeable and easygoing way to study and an excellent way of taking a kind of holiday if you are on your own. The *National Institute of Adult Continuing Education (NIACE)* has a twice-yearly listing of weekend and up to three-week study courses and summer schools. It is published in January and August £1.05 from their office in Leicester.

The *English Tourist Board* publishes an annual guide called

Activity and Hobby Holidays available at bookstalls.

The *Association of British Craftsmen* has a scheme aimed at more serious students of crafts ranging from jewellery design to embroidery and pottery or weaving. Pupils become guests in the craftperson's own home and have the opportunity to work closely with the expert and be taught, probably on a one-to-one/two basis. The scheme can include complete beginners, but also those who have a good knowledge of the craft and want an uplifting 'top up'. Write to them at their office in Bristol.

The arts are covered well in residential courses and many take place in local art centres and workshops. Look for details in magazines or contact your Regional Arts Association. You can get the address from the local library. Many craft courses are covered in the outlets already mentioned.

RADIO AND TELEVISION

There is a continuing range of educational material broadcast through radio and television. A good look through *TV Times* and *Radio Times* will prove fruitful.

Open University programmes are run in conjunction with their study courses and are relayed regularly, though not always at convenient times if you have a family to care for.

Some local radios have educational advice lines, the best known probably being Capital Radio's Helpline. Telephone your local station to see what they offer.

To find out what is planned through the BBC, get the *Radio Times* supplement *Learning at Home* which is published three times a year and lists what will be broadcast or relayed on television during the coming months, or write to *BBC Publications Ltd*.

For ITV write to the Education Officer of your local television company and look through *TV Times,* or write to *ITV Publications Ltd*.

Educational programmes are often accompanied by back-up books available from the publications unit or in special displays in larger book stores. Some are published by independent publishers, but frequently *BBC Publications* or *ITV*

Companies produce their own. Write to them for their catalogues.

Channel 4 produces a lot of educational material, and it has a special responsibility to cater for specialist interests. For more information write to the Educational Liasion Officer at *Channel 4 TV*.

CORRESPONDENCE COURSES

This is a long-established way of studying and it is still a popular method of learning.

Its main advantage is that it is extremely flexible and you can study when you want, although unless you set yourself disciplined targets you are unlikely to finish the course.

The second great advantage is that there are no requirements regarding previous education – no O- or A-levels are required nor are there any age limitations except that you should be over sixteen and have finished full-time education.

Some correspondence colleges advertise aggressively, but you should look for one that is accredited by the *Council for the Accreditation of Correspondence Colleges (CACC)*. This body inspects the colleges, and if it meets their standards, the college will show the appropriate certificate on its prospectus.

Traditional correspondence colleges used to be mainly about passing exams but now include a variety of leisure courses. You will be provided with your own individual timetable and sent lessons at regular intervals. They will normally recommend a book list.

There will be regular assignments that you send to the tutor for marking, but it will be done by correspondence and it may be difficult to speak on the phone or to get face-to-face interviews though some colleges now have telephone contact with tutors. CACC has an advisory service for students and its members have an agreed code of conduct to maintain standards.

Some correspondence colleges now supply courses on tapes and sometimes video tapes. The main disadvantage of studying by correspondence is that it is extremely lonely, although this has now been overcome by various flexible study methods.

Flexistudy is the registered trade name of a scheme devised by the *National Extension College (NEC)*. It is a method whereby you sign on for the course at a local college and have your own tutor whom you can see by appointment. The centre buys the correspondence courses from the NEC but you operate through your local college. You can work as fast or as slowly as you wish, but it does give you the opportunity to have face-to-face meetings with a tutor. Often seminars and meetings where you can meet other students are arranged.

Other colleges or adult education centres have similar systems but are called by different names, such as distance or open learning.

Open Learning has been a major new training initiative from the government-sponsored *Manpower Services Commission (MSC)*. Its aim is to offer opportunities for updating skills to people who, for various reasons, cannot undertake more formal courses of training.

It is an ideal form of learning for women who have been out of the workforce while they were bringing up their families and now wish to return to their previous jobs. Secretaries, for instance, will find that the office has changed significantly in the last few years, and to compete successfully with younger applicants they may need to have word-processing and computing skills.

Home workers find it difficult to get access to training as do many part-time workers, as employers are reluctant to fund such schemes.

If you need to combine working with domestic responsibilities, you may find it difficult to take time to go to conventional evening classes or attend residential courses, and here again, open learning could provide the key.

The system is based on a variety of training materials such as books, video and audio tapes, computer programs etc, which have been created especially for this type of learning. The student is taken through the subject step by step, and there are frequent mini-tests so that you can measure your progress. The programme seems to work best when there is an opportunity to join a network of open learners so that you can provide your own support group. The Open Tech programme, which had been running for five years, ended in March 1987, but the network it set up will continue. Support from colleges or training centres is given but you are expected to be self-motivating, which can prove difficult in some cases.

In September 1987 the Open College was introduced. It provides non-degree-level courses to help people improve their job skills. The courses are available from existing bodies and will lead, if the student wishes, to a credit or a qualification consistent with the proposed *National Council for Vocational Qualifications*.

The idea, still in its early stage, is that students will enrol at a training centre close to home or even at their place of work (if there is one) so that they will receive counselling and support as well as practical facilities where needed and a continuing assessment of their work.

This is only one of the many opportunities offered by the MSC. The Management Extension Programme is a scheme where unemployed managers are introduced to small businesses where their expertise is needed. Each programme lasts for sixteen weeks, and during that time you are paid a weekly training allowance, and in some cases, you can claim travelling expenses.

During the first stage you will take part in a three-week, full-time training course that covers the special problems of small-business management. Following that, you will be seconded to a small firm where you will work on a specific project. Individual programmes are run throughout the country. Each one caters for around twelve managers. For more details ask at your nearest Area Office of the MSC Training Division.

The Wider Opportunities Training Programme arranges full- and part-time courses in line with local employment needs and is designed to help anyone whose skills need updating. It is particularly helpful for women who want to return to work after years at home. It gives you a chance to try out a range of skills to see which are most likely to suit your own aptitudes. Find out more at your local Jobcentre.

The Job Training Scheme replaced the TOPS scheme, and it provides training in skills which will help you get a better job. It can help you improve a skill you have already, or teach you a new one.

Courses generally last from three to six months, although some last up to a year. Most of them are full time. Courses are held at local colleges, government skill centres or on employers' premises.

Training is free, and you will receive an allowance while training – the amount depends upon your personal circumstances and is explained fully in an allowance leaflet which you will be given when you apply. To find out which courses are available in your area, enquire at your local Jobcentre. To be eligible you must be unemployed on the day you start, be over eighteen years of age and have been away from full-time education for at least two years.

The Training for Enterprise Scheme assists those who want to become self-employed or start up small businesses.

The self-employment programme is also ideal for those who are already working for themselves and would like to develop their existing knowledge.

Starting a Small Business extends the basic knowledge to cover legislation regarding employing people and finding and renting accommodation. Full-time courses provide around fifteen days tuition, followed by about five weeks during which you carry out market research and start your business but can keep in touch with programme organisers for regular reviews.

For more details of both programmes, plus a further course, Setting up a Major Business Venture, contact the Adult Training Team at your nearest MSC VET (Vocational Education and Training) Division Area Office. Anyone under 65 (and over eighteen) years of age, whether in employment or unemployed can apply. The MSC is also funding adult training in tourism projects and this includes small-business courses specifically for the hotel and catering industry. For more details contact regional tourist boards (see Address List at the end of Chapter 10, A Chance to Travel) and the MSC VET Division Area Offices.

Don't ever feel that you are too old to join classes. The myth that surrounded our passage into later life once decreed that you were passed learning, along with everything else, once you were over 40, let alone 50 or 60 or 70. Mercifully this has now been largely disproved. It may take you a little longer to grasp new facts but you can probably understand them more easily because you have been around and seen life and gained experience.

There's a lot to be said for joining normal classes along with every other age range. It may take you a week or so to get used to sitting next to a young man with a Mohican haircut, but once you have both got used to the idea, you will find most young people very friendly, if you are, and soon they will be asking your advice and inviting you to coffee without a second thought.

You will be able to join most courses, but not those specifically aimed at training for jobs, unless you can prove you intend to work for a reasonable period afterwards.

Some opportunities are aimed specifically at older people. There are pre-retirement courses throughout the country. You may have been sent on one by your firm, but if not, ask your local Adult Education Centre if it runs one.

Age Concern promotes the education of elderly people through their Forum on the Rights of Elderly People to Education (FREE). It offers a clearing-house on information about education in later years. It brings together people involved or concerned about educational opportunities for older people and acts as a pressure group. Write to FREE for more information.

The *University of the Third Age (U3A)* is the umbrella for self-help learning groups of older people throughout the country. It seeks to involve participants with teaching as well as learning. All groups manage themselves, decide their own activities and raise any necessary funds. It takes just one person with strong motivation to encourage others and get a local group going.

A list of all groups and other information is available from the Executive Secretary. Please enclose a 6 x 10in s.a.e.

The *Workers' Educational Association (WEA)* is a national independent body that runs classes throughout the country. It covers a very wide range of subjects at evening or day classes. It is open to anyone beyond school-leaving age.

Categories covered include basic education, women's

studies, politics, philosophy, history, music and literature, to name a few. The standard of teaching is usually high, but classes are not constrained by examinations and a syllabus leading to formal qualifications.

You can become a member either automatically, by joining a class, or by individual subscription. To find out what is on in your area, contact your local branch. Ask for details at your local library or write to the national head office of WEA.

The *National Adult School Organisation (NASO)* is an umbrella for self-help education groups that meet all over the country. Groups run their own programme, and have elected officers such as chairman, secretary and treasurer. NASO publishes a handbook which suggests how to get a group going in your area and how to run it. They issue discussion leaflets and handbooks and recommend an annual study and discussion subject for which a handbook is available upon which the programme can be based. The study and discussion subject for 1987, for example, was security.

Groups can get together for regional activities which can include residential weekends and social outings. Members are kept in touch through a monthly magazine called *One and All*. There is a small membership fee. Write to NASO for more details.

Educational Counselling and Credit Transfer Information Service (ECCTIS) is a national information service through which you can find out about further and higher education courses all over the country. The levels of study covered are post-graduate, first degree, Higher National Diploma or Certificate, City and Guilds and RSA. They don't cover information about courses of less than six weeks full-time duration (or the part-time equivalent). At the moment the service is free. They also produce a Directory of Educational Guidance Services for adults which should list your local information source, if there is one.

To enable them to give information quickly, it is suggested that you narrow down likely subjects as precisely as possible, indicate the level of study – whether full- or part-time or distance learning – and where you prefer to study. They will also help you with information if you hope to take a course without having the normal entry requirements, and whether previous qualifications can lead to a credit. For more information write to or phone the ECCTIS Information Centre.

For a comprehensive book on all aspects of adult education and training opportunities, you will find all you ever wanted to know (and probably more) in the *National Extension College*'s book *Second Chances* available from them, post paid, at £9.95. Write to the NEC Publications Division.

OPEN UNIVERSITY

The chance to study for a degree regardless of previous qualifications such as O- and A-levels is probably the best known aspect of the *Open University* courses.

Students study from home in their own time, and do most of their work through special study books and assignments, audio cassettes, radio and television broadcasts or video, plus attendance at a summer school for one week on some courses.

To obtain a degree, you need six credits made up of full or half credits depending on the subjects chosen. Although each credit course must be completed within a certain time, you can take as long as you want to notch up six. Each full credit will take approximately nine months and require some twelve to fourteen hours of study a week. Courses begin in February, but applications must be made considerably earlier, and you may have to wait a year before you can be accepted. The earlier you apply, the more chance you have of getting a place.

More than 120,000 people will be currently studying with the Open University. Some will be studying to join the 80,000 people who have already gained Open University degrees and others will be studying single courses, diploma or study packs as associate students in the Programme of Continuing Education.

Continuing Education courses are wide-ranging. There are some to help you in your career or develop personal interests as well as family and community courses. There are 215 subjects to choose from, ranging from Art History, Computing, Education, Family and the Community to Psychology.

Some subjects can be studied with no previous knowledge,

while others will assume that you know a good deal.

Some of the courses can be started at any time of year, but most, especially the longer courses, have closing dates for applications. Fees vary widely and you may get some help from your local authority. It is always worth enquiring, but make sure you get your facts together first before you make approaches.

Open University degrees are as good as any other but it has taken some employers a little longer to accept them. Now many employers sponsor their staff by paying tuition and/or summer school fees or offering time off for summer school, particularly where courses are work-related.

Depending on your interest, send for Guide for Applicants for BA Degree Courses to the Admissions Office, Open University, PO Box 48, Milton Keynes, MK7 6AB, or for details of the Continuing Education programme to Open Opportunities for Continuing Education, Associate Student Central Office, Open University, PO Box 76, Milton Keynes MK7 6AN.

Open Business School

The Open University Open Business School was started in 1983 and has already attracted over 11,500 registrations. It offers the opportunity to study management techniques while still working, and many employees find that their firms are willing to sponsor them.

There are a number of short courses available, or various modules can be put together to qualify for the Open University Diploma in Management. For this there are a number of compulsory components which include Accounting and Finance, The Effective Manager, Marketing in Action and a project. The remaining subjects can be put together to suit your particular aims and needs. The diploma itself involves around 840 hours of study in total.

There are many shorter courses including Managing People, Personnel Selection and Interviewing and a special course on Starting Up Your Own Business.

For this particular course about 50 hours of study are involved, depending a little on the business you have chosen.

It is designed for aspirants who have clear ideas of the types of product or service they want to provide. It is particularly suitable for people in mid-career who want to be their own bosses, redundant executives and people retiring early.

You have contact with a personal adviser for up to nine months. The adviser will be someone with small-business experience. The highlight of the course will be the chance to present your business plan to a panel of business experts.

At the end of the course you will receive a Statement of Course Participation, provided you have submitted your business plan to your adviser.

There is a limited number of sponsored places available. For details write to Startup Project Officer, Open Business School, Walton Hall, Milton Keynes, MK7 6AA. For general queries about Open Business School contact the Regional Enquiry Service at your local Open University Regional Centre or the Customer Services Dept at the address above.

Regional Centres are situated as follows:

UNIVERSITY ADDRESSES

Walton Hall

The Open University's headquarters are at Walton Hall, Milton Keynes, in Buckinghamshire, where the central academic and administrative staff are based. The following box numbers and postcodes should be used when writing on specific matters.

Admission and registration in the Undergraduate Programme:
The Undergraduate Admissions Office
The Open University
PO Box 48
Milton Keynes MK7 6AB

Admission and registration in the Continuing Education Programme:
The Associate Student Central Office
The Open University
PO Box 76
Milton Keynes MK 7 6AN

Admission and registration in the Postgraduate Programme:
The Higher Degree Office
The Open University
PO Box 49
Milton Keynes MK7 6AD

General credit exemptions and credit transfer:
Advanced Standing Office
The Open University
PO Box 80
Milton Keynes MK7 6AS

Purchase of books, films and any other course material:
Open University Education Enterprises
12 Cofferidge Close
Stony Stratford
Milton Keynes MKll 1BY

Other correspondence unless otherwise stated in the Guide should be addressed to:
The Student Enquiries Office
The Open University
PO Box 71
Milton Keynes MK7 6AG

Regional Centres and Study Centres

The University's regional structure is shown on the map on page 79. Regional Centres provide local services for enquirers, applicants and students. Each student is attached to one of the thirteen Regional Centres.

When you fill in your application form you are asked to refer to the list of study centres on the following pages and choose the one most convenient for you (irrespective of where you live). The University will regard your region as that in which your study centre is located.

As demand and availability of premises vary, it may be

necessary to make some changes in the study centres listed before the end of 1988.

If you have immediate questions, however, please do not hesitate to contact the Regional Enquiry Service at your nearest Regional Centre or sub-office.

REGION 01 LONDON
The Open University
London Region
Parsifal College
527 Finchley Road
LONDON NW3 7BG
Tel 01-794 0575

Area covered:
Greater London

Study centres:

Acton W3	008
Bloomsbury WC1	002
Carshalton	022
City (Angel) EC1	227
Cranford	016
Croydon	007
Eltham SE9	228
Enfield (Southgate) N14	010
Harrow	012
Havering	014
Hendon NW4	001
Kingston	017
Mile End E1	020
Norwood SE19	233
Orpington	005
Paddington NW1	235
Pimlico SW1	238
Strand WC2	229
Tottenham N17	011
Twickenham	021
Wandsworth SW15	237
West Hampstead NW3	226

REGION 02 SOUTH

The Open University
Southern Region
Foxcombe Hall
Boars Hill
OXFORD OX1 5HR
Tel 0865 730731

Sub-office:
Winchester
Tel 0962 67969

Area covered:
Berkshire, Buckinghamshire, Channel Islands, Dorset, Hampshire, Isle of Wight, Oxfordshire, part of Wiltshire

Study centres:
Abingdon	025
Aylesbury	026
Banbury	027
Basingstoke	028
Bournemouth	030
Bracknell	031
Fareham	305
Farnborough	037
Guernsey CI	306
High Wycombe	040
Jersey CI	303
Maidenhead	054
Milton Keynes	029
Newbury	041
Newport IOW	042
Oxford (Headington)	043
Poole	044
Portsmouth	045
Reading	046
Salisbury	048
Slough	049
Southampton	050

Weymouth	053
Winchester	035
Witney	055

REGION 13 SOUTH EAST
The Open University
South East Region
Wyvern House
230/232 London Road
EAST GRINSTEAD RH19 1LA
Tel 0342 27821

Answering service:
Tel 0342 26509

Area covered:
Kent, Surrey, East Sussex, West Sussex

Study centres:
Brighton	004
Broadstairs	023
Camberley	032
Canterbury	006
Chichester	033
Crawley	034
Dartford	287
Eastbourne	292
Ewell	036
Folkestone	291
Gillingham	018
Guildford	038
Maidstone	288
Redhill	047
St Leonards-on-Sea	013
Staines	051
Tonbridge	024
Weybridge	052
Worthing	056

REGION 03 SOUTH WEST

The Open University
South West Region
41 Broad Street
BRISTOL BS1 2EP
Tel 0272 299641

Sub-office:
Plymouth
Tel 0752 28321

Area covered:
Avon, Cornwall, Devon, Gloucestershire, Somerset, Scilly
Isles, most of Wiltshire

Study centres:

Barnstaple	057
Bath	058
Bristol (Clifton)	060
Bristol (Fishponds)	295
Cheltenham	063
Chippenham	064
Exeter	065
Gloucester	066
Plymouth	067
Redruth	068
St Austell	069
Swindon	071
Taunton	072
Torquay	073
Weston-super-Mare	074
Yeovil	075

REGION 04 WEST MIDLANDS

The Open University
West Midlands Region
66-68 High Street
Harborne
BIRMINGHAM B17 9NB
Tel 021-426 1661

Area covered:
Hereford and Worcester, Shropshire, most of Staffordshire, Warwickshire, West Midlands

Study centres:

Birmingham (Harbourne)	076
Birmingham (Selly Oak)	091
Coventry	078
Dudley	079
Hereford	080
Kidderminster	082
Leamington Spa	083
Newcastle under Lyme	090
Nuneaton	084
Redditch	085
Rugby	086
Shrewsbury	087
Solihull	088
Stafford	089
Sutton Coldfield	092
Telford	093
Walsall	094
Wolverhampton	095
Worcester	096

REGION 05 EAST MIDLANDS

The Open University
East Midlands Region
The Octagon
143 Derby Road
NOTTINGHAM NG7 1PH
Tel 0602 473072

Area covered:
Most of Derbyshire, Leicestershire, Lincolnshire, Northamptonshire, Nottinghamshire, South Humberside, part of Staffordshire (Burton-on-Trent)

Study centres:

REGION 06 EAST ANGLIA

The Open University
East Anglian Region
Cintra House
12 Hills Road
CAMBRIDGE CB2 1PF
Tel 0223 64721

Area covered:
Bedfordshire, Cambridgeshire, Essex, Hertfordshire, Norfolk, Suffolk

Study centres:

REGION 07 YORKSHIRE
The Open University
Yorkshire Region
Fairfax House
Merrion Street
LEEDS LS2 8JU
Tel 0532 444431

Area covered:
North Humberside, North Yorkshire, South Yorkshire, West
Yorkshire

Study Centres:

REGION 08 NORTH WEST

The Open University
North West Region
Chorlton House
70 Manchester Road
Chorlton-cum-Hardy
MANCHESTER M21 1PQ
Tel 061-861 9823

Area covered:
Cheshire, part of Derbyshire (High Peak area), Isle of Man,
Lancashire, Greater Manchester, Merseyside

Study centres:

Stockport	176
Warrington	177
Wigan	179
Wirral (Birkenhead)	155

REGION 09 NORTH
The Open University
North Region
Eldon House, Regent Centre
Gosforth
NEWCASTLE UPON TYNE NE3 3PW
Tel 091-284 1611

Resource centres:
Cumbria (Penrith)
Tel 0768 64720
Cleveland (Middlesbrough)
Tel 0642 816227

Area covered:
Cleveland, Cumbria, Durham, Northumberland, Tyne and Wear

Study centres:

Ashington	181
Berwick*	251
Carlisle	182
Darlington	183
Durham	184
Furness	154
Gateshead	185
Hartlepool	186
Kendal	324
Newcastle	187
South Tyneside (Boldon)	189
Sunderland	190
Teesside (Middlesbrough)	191
Tynemouth (North Shields)	193
West Cumbria (Egremont)	192

*Location centre with limited facilities

REGION 10 WALES

The Open University in Wales
24 Cathedral Road
CARDIFF CF1 9SA
Tel 0222 397911

Area covered:
Wales

Study centres:

Abergavenny	263
Abergele	197
Aberystwyth	194
Bangor (Menai Centre)	195
Barry	254
Bridgend	255
Cardiff	196
Flint	299
Harlech	257
Haverfordwest	259
Llandrindod	300
Merthyr Tydfil	198
Neath	260
Newport (Gwent)	199
Newtown	262
Pontypridd	264
Swansea	201
Wrexham	203

REGION 11 SCOTLAND

The Open University in Scotland
60 Melville Street
EDINBURGH EH3 7HF
Tel 031-226 3851

Sub-office:
Glasgow
Tel 041-332 4364

Area covered:
Scotland

Study centres:

Aberdeen	204
Arran*	689
Ayr	205
Benbecula*	691
Campbeltown*	692
Clydebank	268
Cowal and Bute*	688
Cumbernauld	270
Dornoch*	687
Dumfries	206
Dundee	207
Edinburgh (Napier)	209
Elgin	274
Falkirk	211
Fort William*	693
Fraserburgh*	686
Galashiels	275
Glasgow (College of Tech)	315
Glasgow (Queen's Coll)	316
Glasgow (Langside)	318
Greenock	276
Hamilton	217
Inverness	215
Islay and Jura*	690
Kirkcaldy	261
Kirkwall* (Orkney)	694
Lerwick* (Shetland)	695
Newton Stewart*	696
Oban*	697
Paisley	218
Perth	279
Skye*	698
Stirling	219
Stornoway*	699
Thurso	281

* Location centres with limited facilities

REGION 12 NORTHERN IRELAND

The Open University in Northern Ireland
40 University Road
BELFAST BT7 1SU
Tel 0232 245025

Area covered:
Northern Ireland

Study centres:
Armagh	220
Ballymena	221
Belfast	223
Coleraine	282
Enniskillen	320
Londonderry	224
Newtownabbey	319
Newtownards	222
Omagh	283

WESTERN EUROPE

Study centres in West Germany and Cyprus are available only for those students admitted under the special scheme for servicemen. The Regional Centres indicated below are those responsible for administering these overseas schemes.

West Germany
(Administered by Region 04)
Bielefeld	410
Hohne	411
Rheindahlen	412
Berlin	413

Cyprus
(Administered by Region 07)
Akrotiri	400
Ayios Nikolaos	401

Belgium and Luxembourg
(Administered by Region 09)
The Open University operates a special scheme for residents of
Belgium and Luxembourg which enables them to study foun-
dation courses and most post-foundation courses. Further
information is available from the North Region Centre in
Newcastle.

Brussels   420

HOW TO STUDY EFFECTIVELY

If you have not undertaken any form of learning for many
years, you may find it surprisingly difficult to knuckle down.
Some people find they can't assimilate what they are taught,
they feel their memories are letting them down or they cannot
read fast enough to keep up with the course. Relax. These are
techniques that you can rediscover.

If you are embarking on a long course of learning for a qualification or a degree course, you would be advised, if not specifically asked, to take a pre-learning course which will reintro-
duce you to the techniques of study.

Once you have left school, what you learn is largely up to
you. You educate yourself from available resources. No-one
can make you learn or keep you behind to write lines or reassess
a passage from a book. The effort must be your own, and a correspondence course, or your tutor, will help you discover the
resources available, or at least point you in the right direction.

Effective Reading

The list of books you will be expected to delve into may seem
overwhelming at first. Some will be very much more useful
than others. Your first task will be to analyse which books will
be of the most value and to put them into some kind of order
of priority.

Categorise each book, and don't forget to identify each one
with the title, publisher and author. Make brief notes about
what each book will contain. You can normally do this by

05 denotes O.U. Region

BELFAST■ denotes O.U. Regional Office

▲ Education and Library Boards are shown for N. Ireland

reading the contents carefully and dipping into chapters to check that the tone of the book is in line with your research. It is important to follow this procedure, as sometimes what seems in theory to be the perfect book is too intellectual in approach or, conversely, for too popular a market to be of use to you.

There will be very few occasions when you need to read a book word by word. In general you can afford to skim and just go back to reread some of the paragraphs or pages. You will find that some chapters are relevant and others less so, so don't feel you must plough through them all. It is not necessary to read each paragraph word by word. Try to speed up your reading by skipping words or reading down the middle of a page rather than right out to the edges.

If you find that you frequently don't understand the meaning of something, it might be time to increase your vocabulary. Whatever you do, don't just skip the word; find out what it means by keeping a good dictionary on hand.

Although it is important to absorb what you read, it is also vital to keep an open mind on what the authors are saying. Do you really agree with their views? How could you support an opposite one? By keeping a degree of detachment, you will learn to make up your own mind about ideas and statements, and develop your own views and theories instead of coming up with secondhand thoughts.

A Place to Study

It is important to have your own private place to study if you possibly can. A haven of your own where you can sit comfortably and quietly and where you can leave books open without fear of them being disturbed. If background noise or other distractions are likely to be a problem, you could consider a pair of earplugs. It helps if you can make it the same place week after week, so that by actively going and sitting down you will have prepared yourself to work. Make it as easy for yourself as possible. A comfortable chair and a good light are essential. You will need some kind of table or desk, somewhere for your books and pens. Keep it as far away from the rest of the family as you can. A bedroom often works well if it can be heated. If you are too cold, you will find it hard to study and if too hot, you will fall asleep over your books.

You are bound to acquire a good deal of filing during your study, so decide how you will keep it – in card folders, plastic sheets, a ring binder – then set about making an index so that you can find what you want as quickly as possible.

A typewriter will be a bonus when it comes to preparing essays. Anything that makes your work easier to read from a tutor's as well as your own point of view is always a blessing.

Take Effective Notes

Good notes will be your aide-mémoire. Any notes you take will be to help your memory, so you can write in your own personal shorthand or however you like, as long as it will convey something to you when the time comes to reread them.

Good notes are usually concise. If they take too long to write at the time, you will miss the point of the lecture or what you are reading. They must sum up the points made, or direct you to the source of reference quickly. Write things in your own words, don't copy anyone else's phrase. By putting things in your special language it will help you to understand the subject.

If you are taking notes at a lecture don't try to write down too much. It is already difficult enough to really listen to what is being said without giving yourself the extra difficulty of writing copious notes at the same time. If you can train yourself to listen without distractive thoughts ruining your concentration, you should find it is sufficient to take sparse notes at the time, then at the end of the day go over what you have written and amplify it if you need to. In any case you will probably need to tidy up what you have jotted down. It may be worthwhile making a brief synopsis of the lecture at this point.

ADDRESS LIST

Age Concern, Bernard Sunley House, 60 Pitcairn Road, Mitcham, Surrey CR4 3LL. 01 640 5431

Association of British Craftsmen, 57 Coombe Bridge Avenue, Stoke Bishop, Bristol BS9 2LT. 0272 686417

BBC Books, Woodlands, 80 Wood Lane, London W12 OTT

Channel 4 TV, 60 Charlotte Street, London W1P 2AX

Council for the Accreditation of Correspondence Colleges (CACC), 27 Marylebone Road, London NW1 5JS. 01 935 5391

Educational Counselling and Credit Transfer Information Service (ECCTIS), PO Box 88, Walton Hall, Milton Keynes MK7 6DB. 0908 368921

Educational Programme Services, IBA, 70 Brompton Road, London SW3 1EY. 01 584 7011

English Tourist Board (also British Tourist Authority), Thames Tower, Blacks Road, London W9 9EL. 01 846 9000

Forum on the Rights of Elderly People (FREE), see Age Concern above

ITV Publications Ltd, 247 Tottenham Court Road, London W1F 0AY

Manpower Services Commission, see local telephone directory

National Adult School Organisation (NASO), Norfolk House, Smallbrook, Queensway, Birmingham B5 3LJ. 021 643 9297

National Council for Vocational Qualifications, 222 Euston Rd, London NW1 2BZ. 01–387 9898

National Extension College (NEC), 18 Brooklands Avenue, Cambridge CB2 2HN. 0223 316644

National Institute of Adult Continuing Education (NIACE), 19B De Montfort Street, Leicester LE1 7GE. 0533 551451

Open University, PO Box 76, Milton Keynes MK7 6AN. 0908 74066

– for information on degree courses, Admissions Office,

Open University, PO Box 48, Milton Keynes MK7 6AB.
- for information on Continuing Education courses, Open Opportunities for Continuing Education, Associate Student Central Office, Open University, PO Box 76, Milton Keynes MK7 6AN.
- for information on business studies, Open Business School, Walton Hall, Milton Keynes, MK7 6AA.

U3A, 6 Parkside Gardens, London SW19 5EY

Workers' Educational Association (WEA), 9 Upper Berkeley Street, London W1H 8BY. 01–402 5608/9

4

YOUR TIME FOR FREE

If you have decided that money is no longer a priority, or if you feel that you are unlikely to get paid work for whatever reason, you can become a valued and useful member of one of any number of voluntary organisations that rely on unpaid help.

Whatever your interests, there will be an organisation or self-help group that fosters it. Be it animal welfare, conservation, preservation, child welfare, the elderly, the disabled, consumer rights, there are, within those and many other headings, local and national groups that would welcome your help.

People who shop for housebound neighbours, call on an elderly person who lives nearby or assist at a local jumble sale to raise funds for the third world often don't really regard themselves as doing anything very special. In fact most of us help out in some kind of way, and active volunteering for some kind of social involvement is really an extension of this type of network.

It is the urge to help others in most of us that keeps a myriad of schemes afloat. Even if we never see the recipients, we engage in collecting, fund-raising or campaigning with considerable enthusiasm.

Successful volunteers are usually those who get out of their enterprise as much as they put in, in terms of achievement and satisfaction.

Don't hesitate to offer help just because you feel your true motives are to get to know more people or find an outlet for a particular skill now that you have retired and no-one seems to appreciate you. Very few of us offer to give up several hours a week for purely altruistic reasons, and one could query the motives of those who claim they do.

There is a lot of satisfaction and fun to be found in working together to offer help where it is needed, and to see the fruits materialise in terms of knitted blankets for Africa or presenting a mini-bus to take disabled children on outings.

If you feel a blazing desire to help disadvantaged teenagers, then find, face to face, that you are appalled by their language or behaviour – don't give up. Take a side step and help the cause in an administrative way, or offer to raise funds.

If you are lonely, you can meet people and gradually make friends with other volunteers. It will get you out of the house if you haven't a reason for going. Should you find time hangs heavily while you are job-hunting, or if your employment fails to provide the stimulus you need, the right kind of voluntary work will fill the gap. You may feel you are in lowly unfulfilling work, and what you do as a volunteer is appreciated and can build up your self-esteem.

Motherly ladies, suffering from the empty-nest syndrome, may find satisfaction in caring for children in need or counselling young mothers who can't cope. You may have had a particularly traumatic experience where your own lesson in coping will be of benefit passed on to others anguishing over the same difficulty.

Volunteering doesn't have to be too great a commitment if you don't want it to be. A couple of hours a week is as gratefully received as a couple of days. If you can only help occasionally, that is welcome too.

One thing that will be required is reliability. Don't start anything you can't keep up. Imagine the damage that could be caused to an abandoned child if you didn't turn up for a planned visit, or what would happen if you didn't keep your promise to take a disabled person to the dentist.

One of the most important things is to volunteer for something you enjoy. It's quite easy to be so taken up with the thought of helping that you plunge in and tackle something you don't really care to do. It's rather like taking up swimming as a form of regular exercise when you don't like getting wet.

You can be sure that a sincere desire to help and a firm

commitment will be welcome. This doesn't mean that you just walk in to your nearest branch and are welcomed with open arms. It can take quite a long time to find the right niche – where your own skills and enthusiasm can be tailored to what is needed. You must be flexible, be willing to join a team and be directed, at least up to a point. With such a huge variety of causes and tasks, you can easily pick on one that you can be enthusiastic about. Take time to work out which form your help will take. Talk to anyone you know who is already involved so that you get some idea of what it will be like.

Will you want some person-to-person contact with those you aim to assist? Are you shy and retiring and would you prefer to be a back-room person who operates in an administrative capacity? Are you good with money? Do you have a list of contacts so that the fund-raising side of a venture would appeal?

Be realistic about conditions. Charities are in the business of raising money, so don't expect luxurious offices. Back-up funds will be short for the projects you are working on and resources limited.

The objects of your concern may not be over-appreciative of your efforts, and far from giving profuse thanks may complain volubly. They may not be clean, they may have awful habits or be just plain tiresome. How will you cope with that?

An ideal volunteer has plenty of common sense, is tolerant, flexible and willing to do what is needed at the time. A sense of humour undoubtedly helps.

The most likely way to volunteer is to get involved through other people you know who are already doing it. They may ask you to help out one day when their numbers are short and you can go on from there. If you know who you want to help, you can write to the charity directly and ask to be put in touch with their local network.

Hospitals and social service departments sometimes have volunteer organisers of their own. Hospital visiting, especially in geriatric wards where some long-term patients have no visitors at all, would be appreciated, as would someone willing to wheel the magazine trolley round the wards, or write letters for someone who isn't up to it, or see to the flowers.

The ways you can help an organisation obviously vary to a degree, but there is normally plenty of scope within each one. *The Oxford Committee for Famine Relief (OXFAM)*, for example, publishes a special booklet for those interested in volunteering which is available free on receipt of a large stamped self-addressed envelope. It covers helping at a local office, specialist skills that are welcome – fund raising, campaigning, school and youth workers and helping in their shops. Each aspect is explained in the booklet, and the sort of staff that need to be recruited include secretaries, drivers to collect goods to be sold at OXFAM shops, public speakers, stock controllers, public relations officers, flag day organisers and those who can knit and sew blankets. If you want to work on your own, there is a booklet on fund-raising ideas as well as one on raising money at work. If you help in one of the shops, you could be asked to do anything from sorting what comes in, casting an expert eye over the bric-à-brac, fixing an odd shelf, lettering price cards or helping with the window display. Write for more information.

Other large organisations will have similar structures, while the same skills will still be needed by smaller charities.

Deciding who to help can really be quite difficult if you just have a general desire to do something about those less fortunate than yourself, rather than having a specific goal in mind.

Much volunteering is about people, and categories, if they can be called such, can include children – disadvantaged, sick, mentally handicapped, teenagers, including young offenders. You may get involved in running a crèche, an adventure playground, becoming an 'aunt' or 'uncle', running a holiday play scheme, organising country holidays for deprived youngsters, or taking some in yourself. Don't forget that becoming a Scout, Cub, Brownie or Guide leader is a long-established way of helping the young.

If your concern is for elderly people, assistance can range from becoming a hospital visitor for long-stay patients in geriatric hospitals to taking an interest in the local home for the elderly. You could assist with the Meals on Wheels service, start a Good Neighbour scheme, help at a local Day Centre, take an older person for an afternoon outing in your car, or take one to the chiropodist, help with a holiday scheme run by a charity like *Age Concern* or join their group in your area (or if there isn't one, see if you can start one). As always, your local *Citizens' Advice Bureau* will put you in touch with each group's organisers.

Sick people of all ages need befriending, especially if they don't have relatives or for some reason they cannot visit. Help in mental hospitals can be rewarding, but you need to be prepared for discouragement and be able to rise above it and carry on. If person-to-person contact is not for you, there is a lot of fund- raising work to be done.

The *British Red Cross Society* operates more than 50 welfare services both in hospitals and in the community. They range from escorting housebound people on outings, assisting at clubs and Day Centres, giving speech therapy (under guidance) to victims of strokes, operating toy libraries and organising annual holidays for handicapped and elderly people. These are just a few of the things the Red Cross does, and all need the assistance of volunteers. To find out more of the services given in your area, and where you can help, contact your local branch. Disabled people of all ages, including those who are blind and deaf, have many associations and societies that attempt to look after their needs, and they all need volunteers. If you cannot undertake a regular commitment you might be able to help at a holiday home, or assist with driving when an outing is planned.

Counselling is an overused and sometimes misused word today, and, it is easy to dismiss the many wonderful schemes that it covers. Whatever your problem, you will find there is a hotline to help – from the other end of a telephone line where a caller can remain anonymous or, where appropriate, a face-to-face meeting with an adviser.

Probably the most famous Helpline of all is the *Samaritans*, where telephone lines are manned 24 hours a day by volunteers who have the backing of paid professional advisers. Centres are also open to visitors on a no appointment, drop-in basis during daytime and evening. To be accepted as a volunteer, you must have a friendly manner, be sympathetic, tolerant and unshockable, and above all, a good listener. At the other end of your telephone will be despairing people in the pit of misery, and you must be able to give support yet not become overburdened yourself. If you are chosen to become a volunteer you will undergo training and serve as a probationer for a year.

To be considered for marriage guidance counselling by the *National Marriage Guidance Council* you will undertake a rigorous vetting. To be accepted you should normally be between 25 and 55 years of age. Men and women are welcomed, the percentage of counsellors at the moment being approximately one third men/two thirds women. Currently there are 1800 but the Council is always looking for more.

It helps if you have some knowledge of working with people, or have experience in one of the caring professions. You are expected to have not too many problems of your own, not to be too judgemental, and in general to have some experience of life. An ideal counsellor would be able to put people at ease and be unshockable.

A commitment of around eight or nine hours a week is expected, and considerable time is spent in training. This consists of part-time involvement over two to two and a half years with six 48-hour sessions at the headquarters in Rugby. Training includes taking part in fortnightly local case discussion groups. Throughout training and afterwards your work is supervised by your own personal marriage guidance tutor. You meet your first clients early on – about three months after you begin. In addition to training there is an extensive booklist to keep up with.

There are many many more counselling schemes available – some small and some large. They may have been born out of traumatic experiences such as a cot death, or may exist to help agoraphobics or gamblers, to name just a few.

The *Citizens' Advice Bureaux (CAB)* are mostly staffed by volunteers who receive professional training before interviewing and advising clients. They have a vast back-up of information which is continually updated. The number of questions they might tackle in any one week may seem daunting until you are in the thick of it, but most CAB workers soon learn to take it in their stride.

Emergency service is undertaken by the *St John Ambulance*

and the *British Red Cross Society* as well as the *Women's Royal Voluntary Service*, to name just three.

Helping isn't necessarily to do with people or even animals. Conservation projects need help too. Although most people think of the tasks as just for young people, if you are able-bodied and willing to fit in, you will be welcome to help clear paths, build dry-stone walls and dredge lakes. The *British Trust for Conservation Volunteers* will send you more details. The *Inland Waterways Association* campaigns for the restoration, retention and development of inland waterways in the British Isles and their fullest commercial and recreational use. Its associated *Waterway Recovery Group* is pleased to hear of volunteers to help with restoration work at weekends in certain parts of the country. The *Council for the Protection of Rural England* needs 'ears' everywhere to give warning of unsuitable development plans or any other threats to the countryside. The *Nature Conservancy Council*, whose brief includes looking after nature reserves, needs enthusiastic volunteers to work with their full-time officers.

You may think that you should look after the town or city in which you live before you venture outside, in which case join your local preservation society or tenants' association. You can find out if they exist by looking for notices in the local library or ask at your Town Hall. The *Civic Trust* is an umbrella organisation to which many local societies are affiliated. You may have an Historical Society, there may be an amenity group, but all will be channelled to improving your own local environment, a task which is an uphill struggle at best.

If you read your local paper regularly, you will soon get to know the charities and pressure groups that are active in your area.

Many towns have a volunteer bureau whose aim is to match the job to be done with a suitable person to do it. The telephone number is in the yellow pages or ask your local *Citizens' Advice Bureau*, then ring up and make an appointment to drop in for a chat. They will try hard to find the right niche for you.

The Volunteer Centre is a national agency advising on voluntary work. It aims to put prospective helpers in touch with local groups. The normal procedure is for anyone wishing to help to drop in to the Centre offices for a chat. Look for your local one in the phone book or write to the national office.

The *Retired Executives Action Clearing House (REACH)* matches retired executives with voluntary organisations who need those business skills. Their service is free of charge. REACH is not an employment agency, and deals only with charities or voluntary organisations, so it cannot find you paid work, although expenses, such as travelling, will normally be met.

Depending on where you live, you may find more positions vacant than volunteers to fill them. In Greater London, for example, there is the difficulty of finding sufficient volunteers because so many charities operate from London, while in remote rural areas, such as some parts of East Anglia, there may be more volunteers than vacancies.

Anyone with financial expertise is especially welcome and so are people offering communication skills – in public relations, marketing or in general organisation – to name just some functions. You need to be flexible and willing to adapt to new circumstances if you are thinking of volunteering.

No-one is going to give you exactly the job you were doing as a paid professional, but the plus point is that you will not be under the same pressures and will be able to work more at your own pace.

The real value is that working gives you a sense of belonging and a commitment. It ensures that you remain useful and mentally alert.

It is important that you link up with an organisation that has aims with which you can feel sympathy and enthusiasm, and with such a vast range on offer that cannot be difficult.

A 53-year-old former WRNS officer, for example, who was living at West Mersea in Essex was looking for work with a horticultural flavour. She is now happily engaged in organising a fund-raising, gardens-opening scheme in Essex. A 50-year-old south London woman who had spent 21 years with a large bank, the last four as personnel manager, accepted the post of honorary secretary to the *Turner Society*, set up to further the appreciation and study of Britain's famous painter.

A former company chairman is acting as consultant to the group director of marketing and communications of the *Royal Society for Mentally Handicapped Children and Adults (MENCAP)*.

Once you have decided what you would like to do and nominated an association or two to contact, you will probably end up sitting opposite an organiser with an opportunity to find out more. This is the time to keep your eyes and ears open and work out whether you think you will like the people with whom you are going to be involved. Even the best project goes sour if you cannot identify with the group. If their business overwhelms you or their lack of organisation is irksome, look for other avenues. It's got to feel right for the connection to be a success.

Enquire about what kind of tasks they have in mind for you. Does anyone ask what you would like to do or is it taken for granted that you will address the envelopes for ever? Being willing to do anything to help is one thing but not if it stifles your interest before you get going.

A well-run group will have objectives and a plan of operation. The team will know what it is doing, and even more important, why. If you are going to offer your precious time, you will want to know that it is going to be put to good effect and not turn out to be the equivalent of a gossipy coffee morning.

Do people in the group appear to get on well with each other or can you sense tensions? Is it your impression that they get on well with other interrelated associations or is there a hint of rivalry or hostility in the air? Unfortunately groups of all kinds fall prey to negative attitudes, and it would be senseless to join such a team.

Will you receive any training or support at the beginning and/or once you are out on your own? Training can encompass many things from a couple of hours discussion to proper classroom courses, but you will certainly operate better if someone has sat down with you and at least attempted to show you the ropes. Perhaps you can sit in on some discussions or go out with an existing helper when he/she visits an elderly person or supervises at an adventure playgroup or runs a committee meeting.

All this advice may seem a far cry from your first tentative step of helping run a coffee morning in a friend's house or giving someone a lift to the dentist but with so much future satisfaction and enjoyment at stake it is worth taking the trouble to find the right niche.

ADDRESS LIST

Age Concern, Bernard Sunley House, 60 Pitcairn Road, Mitcham, Surrey CR4 3LL. 01 640 5431

Age Concern Northern Ireland, 6 Lower Crescent, Belfast BT7 1NR. 0232 245729

Age Concern Scotland, 33 Castle Street, Edinburgh EH2 3DN. 031 225 5000

Age Concern Wales, 1 Park Grove, Cardiff, S. Glamorgan CF1 3BJ. 02222 371566 or 371821

British Red Cross Society, 9 Grosvenor Crescent, London SW1X 7EJ. 01 235 5454

British Trust for Conservation Volunteers, 36 St. Mary's Street, Wallingford, Oxon OX10 0EU. 0491 39766

Children's Society, Edward Rudolf House, Margery Street, London WC1Y 0JL. 01 837 4299

Citizens' Advice Bureau, see local telephone directory or National Association of Citizens' Advice Bureaux below

Civic Trust, 17 Carlton House Terrace, London SW1Y 5AW. 01 930 0914

Council for the Protection of Rural England, 4 Hobart Place, London SW1W 0HY. 01 235 9481

Dr Barnardo's (head office), Tanners Lane, Barkingside, Ilford, Essex LG 6 1QG. 01 550 8822

Girl Guides Association, 17–19 Buckingham Palace Road, London SW1W 0PT. 01 828 1448

Greenpeace UK, 6 Endsleigh Street, London WC1H 0DS. 01 387 5370

Imperial Cancer Research, PO Box 123 Lincolns Inn Fields, London WC2A 3PX. 01 242 0200

Inland Waterways Association, 114 Regent's Park Road, London NW1 8V2. 01 586 2510

MENCAP, see Royal Society for Mentally Handicapped Children and Adults below

National Association of Citizens' Advice Bureaux (CAB), 115–123 Pentonville Road, London N1 9LZ. 01 833 2181

National Council for Voluntary Organisations (NCVO), 26 Bedford Square, London WC1B 3HV. 01 636 4066

National Marriage Guidance Council, Herbert Gray College, Little Church Street, Rugby CV21 3AP. 0788 73241

National Society for the Prevention of Cruelty to Children (NSPCC), 67 Saffron Hill, London EC1N 8RS. 01 242 1626

National Trust, 36 Queen Anne's Gate, London SW1H 9AS. 01 222 9251

Nature Conservancy Council, Northminster House, Peterborough PE1 1UA. 0733 40345

Oxford Committee for Famine Relief (OXFAM), 274 Banbury Road, Oxford OX2 7DZ. 0865 56777

Retired Executives' Action Clearing House (REACH), 89 Southwark Street, London SE1 0HD. 01 928 0452

Royal Society for Mentally Handicapped Children and Adults, 123 Golden Lane, London EC1Y 0RT. 01 253 9433

St John Ambulance, 1 Grosvenor Crescent, London SW1 7ES. 01 235 5231

Samaritans, 17 Uxbridge Road, Slough SL1 1SN. 0753 32713/4

SSAFA

Scouts' Association, Baden-Powell House, Queen's Gate, London SW7 5LQ. 01 584 7030

Volunteer Centre (national office), 29 Lower King's Road, Berkhamsted, Herts HP4 2AB. 04427 73311

Winged Fellowship Trust, Angel House, Pentonville Road, London N1 9XD. 01 833 2594

Women's Royal Voluntary Service, 17 Old Park Lane, London W1Y 4AJ. 01 499 6040

5

WHERE SHALL WE LIVE?

MOVING HOME

The question of moving house is almost bound to come up when retirement is considered. It is also a significant consideration if you have made the decision to change your lifestyle through a career change or enforced redundancy.

Some aspects are more pressing than others if you still have many years of working life left, but the basic considerations are broadly the same. Should you move at all, and if so, where and how should you approach the matter?

Years ago, on retirement, folk would often move to a coastal resort and expect to live happily ever after. Happy holidays in a bustling seaside town did not prepare them for the reality of a rain- and sea-washed promenade in the height of winter when most of the shops and cafés had closed and everyone around them appeared to be older and less active than they were.

Now the subject of retirement is aired more thoroughly, fewer people fall into such a trap, but there are still plenty of pitfalls nevertheless.

Supposing you agree to remain in the same town you have always lived in – whether or not in the same house will be discussed later – you will have to accept the fact that many of your friends may move away.

In short, there is no one correct decision. It is an individual choice that only you and your partner can make, based on what you expect to happen in the years ahead.

If, for example, you plan to take up part-time or voluntary work, you may be as happy staying put as moving to a strange place. On the other hand, those very same ambitions will help you meet new people and encounter new experiences when you uproot.

It is an important decision and one to be taken over a decent period of time. If you fancy another area, make sure you see it in winter as well as in summer. Find out if the area has an average or above average rainfall, whether it feels damp, average hours of sunshine etc.

Another way of anticipating your move ahead would be to change district while you are still at work. Many people do this successfully, although the stress of commuting many miles each day is considerable.

If, for example, you have made the decision to move away from a major city but still within 50 miles or so, you could consider commuting for a few years, providing transport or road access is reasonable. It can give you a chance to get integrated within your new district before you find you are there all day every day with a considerable amount of time on your hands.

> Ann and Harry were both journalists who decided to wind down a little and work less than a full working week. They moved to north Norfolk from London, yet still retained a freelance association with their previous companies. This meant that they worked partly from their new home and partly by commuting 100 miles or more and back at regular intervals.
>
> Fortunately, they still had plenty of friends in the city, so that when necessary they could stay overnight. They also made an arrangement with their firms to pay their fares, so all they really had to supply for themselves was the extra travelling time.
>
> At the same time they have joined in various local activities and taken an interest in amenity societies and so have gradually extended their nucleus of friends. They are now happily integrated in their new

life and can relinquish London ties gradually or totally whenever they wish.

Maggie and Tom were teachers, just in their fifties when they decided to take the plunge and move 50 miles away from their school. They benefited considerably in being able to buy a brand new high-quality home in a pleasant small country town at a more reasonable price than if they had stayed in London. Because they worked together, and had good parking facilities at school, they were able to drive in and out together and share the driving. Even so, they found it extremely tiring, but now, one year later, they believe it has worked out in their favour.

When your move is associated with a new job you have extra considerations that must be taken into account.

The difficulty for anyone living in the north finding accommodation in the south is well documented. Before you uproot your family, it is wise to make sure that you are going to settle in your new job. If you own your house it may be better to delay selling it and moving away for a few months until you know your move is likely to be at least reasonably permanent.

However, it isn't only the north/south divide that needs careful thought and planning. Moving to a prosperous town or a picture village anywhere may mean that accommodation is more expensive. Proceed with caution.

CHECK THE AMENITIES

Investigate whether your chosen location has the amenities you need or may need in the future – good medical facilities, sufficient entertainment, adequate transport. Some places just have a better 'feel' than others and you may not be able to identify it more closely than that.

Whatever may have attracted you in the first place, now is the time to take a step back and have a long hard look. What sort of shops are there? Are the prices what you are used to or is every item just more expensive? In a month's shopping, a penny or two on each item will add up to quite a sum. Visit the local pubs and see if you like the people; wander up and down the streets, sit in the local park. Over a few visits you will soon know whether you really feel at home or not.

See whether there are facilities to take up hobbies, either current or ones you hope to enjoy. The local library will reveal all, or certainly nearly all, and so will a glance at the adverts on shop boards or in the local paper.

Buy large-scale maps of the area and study them well, so that when you are house-hunting from a distance you will know that one road runs alongside the railway line and another is close to a large park.

Supposing you have received a sizeable sum in redundancy money and have a largish house to sell, you may find the idea of cashing in, and investing your money to live on (see more on page 134) makes moving into the remoter areas an attractive proposition. In some parts of the country you can pay comparatively little for an attractive house if you are comparing it with London or south of England prices. You could cash in quite handsomely if you choose your area carefully. The difficulty here would be if you ever wanted to reverse your decision and move back – the natural rise in house prices would cut into your investment money to such a degree that it might make the move back impossible.

It is only too easy to be seduced by the vision of a lovely home and garden miles away that gives you enough in the bank after you have bought it to live quietly without working. Reality can be disappointing. Once you have brought the house round to your liking and tidied up the garden, what will you do? Your friends and family are miles away and you don't know many people locally. Are you self-sufficient enough to make out or will it seem a hollow triumph?

All these are questions to ask yourself and to discuss fully with your partner. Many people make such moves and live happily ever after, but they are the ones who have reasoned through such a move.

Pamela and Mac moved from the south-east coast to a pretty house in Herefordshire giving them enough, with Mac's redundancy money, to live quite happily without working. Pamela was an enthusiastic amateur singer and quickly made her mark with a local choir, while Mac was happy at home engrossed in the couple of acres he had acquired and happy to spend most of his time lovingly setting it out as he wanted. Both of them were quite happy with the move in different ways.

THINK AHEAD

Whatever your location, when you look around an area, think ahead to when you may not be as mobile or may give up running a car. What will the facilities seem like then? The winding path down an unmade track to your country retreat may not be the same without a car.

You may feel now that you have no time to enjoy leisure pursuits or the amenities of a community centre, but later that may change. Would you prefer to live within walking distance of the local library, the swimming-pool, the municipal tennis courts, not to mention the bank and post office.

If you enjoy concerts, the theatre or cinema, should you consider living close to or in a town that can offer such facilities? Don't just consider your position now. Try to see yourself and your partner in a few years time, as moving is expensive and you may not want the upheaval of uprooting yourself yet again later on.

GOING TO THE CHILDREN

Should you move house to be nearer your children? For some families the answer is undoubtedly yes. The children are genuinely delighted to have mum and dad nearby, in which case the said mum and dad will almost certainly know the ground rules. Most likely, these will be not to drop in too often, especially unannounced, and never to interfere in squabbles or in decisions about the grandchildren. For anyone considering such a major step there are other considerations.

There is no guarantee that the children will not move again within a few years, with the possibility of leaving you 'stranded' in a new town. Even if you enjoy a happy relationship, they may not be overjoyed at the prospect of having you within such easy reach that you drop in on them too often or they feel guilty if they want to forego a regular Saturday visit to do other things.

The plus points however are many. You can help them in many ways by baby-sitting, if there are children, and thus enjoy seeing your grandchildren grow up. You will also be available to give them treats and take time to listen to them and encourage their interests and hobbies. Active parents can help, and in turn be helped, with home improvements – another pair of hands is always welcome. This mutual help need not be a one-way traffic unless in the past you have made it so. Most families help each other and are accustomed to give and take. If you have a sneaking feeling that you do more giving than taking, you will probably be equally surprised to feel that your children think the same!

You can keep an eye on each other's houses when one family is away on holiday, look after the dog and feed the cat and do other neighbourly things that can be so difficult to organise.

Sometimes you will find yourselves belonging to the same clubs or church, and by meeting their friends too, you can extend your age range of acquaintances, which is always a good idea but not always so easy to achieve.

Many parents have wonderful relationships with their children, built up of love and respect on both sides. But even with the closest relationship, it isn't wise to spend too much of your time with your offspring and rely on them overmuch for your social life and well-being.

COUNTRY LIVING

Country cottages with the statutory roses around the door can be charming. In many villages there exists a genuine community spirit, but much of it is saved for families who have been in the district for many years. If you move into a new housing development on the outskirts for instance, you may find a silent battle between 'them and us' unfolds. Many villages are simply dormitory towns for nearby major cities. Transport can be a problem, and although you may have one or even two cars, it can be extremely frustrating to have to drive five miles to buy a loaf of bread when the village shop is closed or has run out. The local library is eleven miles away and so, probably, is the dry cleaners or the Indian takeaway.

Generally speaking, however, you get out of village life what you put in. If you set about joining in the various associations, offer to help at jumble sales or village fêtes, and frequent the village pub regularly to meet local people, you will eventually fit in without too much trouble, but probably not as quickly as you might think.

Although one of the quickest ways to enter into village life is to have children at the local school, by offering your services and entering into the spirit of the community you will soon have a string of acquaintances, if not friends.

The plus side of life in a small village is that neighbours are usually very kindly if you are ever in trouble – in illness or family crisis. The down side is that if you offend one, you often offend them all, and that no part of your life is ever really private.

Gossip is the life blood of small villages – not malicious – just busybody news keeps most folk going.

Pauline and Richard moved from a London suburb to an East Sussex small town. They didn't know a soul and moved into a close – a clutch of brand new houses and bungalows within walking distance of the centre and the station. Although Richard suffers quite severely with arthritis and uses a walking stick to move around, in only six months they had made lots of friends and acquired an active social life.

Because they had moved into a brand new close, everyone was in the same position and anxious to get to know neighbours. They didn't have to break down cliques of existing, long-standing friendships at least in that network.

Before they moved, they had learned to play bridge at evening school, so that they had a sociable hobby, and it was this as much as anything else that brought them into contact with people in the area.

STAYING PUT

Moving to another district isn't the right decision for everyone. If you have paid attention to your future and built in time during your busy life to take part in activities outside work and family, you will find yourself busy, happy and reluctant to leave the network of friends and acquaintances that have been made so painstakingly during the years. Nevertheless you may find your home is too big, too inconvenient or too expensive to run and there is a need to move.

By staying in the same district you have a distinct advantage. You will know the area extremely well and can bide your time until you come across a property that you may like to consider. You may know of retirement housing that is being built or you may consider a suitable place to rent.

Whatever your decision, you will at least avoid the mistake of not knowing the area sufficiently well to see the snags. You will know only too well if the roads are jam-packed with commuter cars during the weekday or if you can't get in to your garage because of Saturday shoppers at the weekend.

What you can do is take your time to look for a smaller property in a part of the town you like and which may be even better than the one you live in now.

When you do make the change it is prudent perhaps to add extra considerations to your choice. Although you may have always loved the chance to 'do up' a tumbledown house, or been impervious to draughts and damp, you may now find that it is more important to consider your overall comfort in your next choice.

Quite often, people who have always enjoyed living in older property make the choice to move into a brand new house that has been built with all the extra insulation comforts that are now the norm. New properties are much easier to maintain, and if you are around as the house is being built, you can influence some decisions like where the plugs will be fixed on the wall. Very often, new woodwork won't need painting, double glazing is fitted as a standard amenity, all of which is good news unless you are a particularly fiendish DIY buff.

MOBILE HOMES

Mobile or park homes could be the answer to where to live. Compared with a normal house, the costs are considerably less, and if you choose your site well and read the small print of any agreements carefully, you could find the arrangement very satisfactory.

The Mobile Homes Act 1983 gave tenants more protection than previously and went quite a way to offset the previous drawbacks which caused so much bad publicity.

There is now protection against eviction and guidelines on how you can sell your home on its site. You are not obliged to sell it to the site owner, though you must seek his consent to the sale.

If you bring your own new home to a site, you will pay for the installation and connection of services as well as the landscaping of your own plot. After that you will pay ground rent and rates together with water rates. If you buy an existing home already on a site you will not have to pay connection charges.

At 40 Lynn lived in a mobile home for two years after her marriage broke up. She was extremely happy and only sold it when she moved from the area and would certainly consider doing the same again.

On her site she found there was a good age mix of people, although there were more people in their fifties or retired than younger, and more couples than single people.

Lynn's home included a single bedroom, and a great plus as far as she was concerned, an open fire. The fuel was kept in a coal bunker outside next to the storage shed provided for every home on site.

When Lynn came to sell up she sold the home privately, but paid the site owner ten per cent. She also found she paid 2 or 3p a unit extra for electricity while she was there, but apart from that found the out-goings reasonable. Her ground rent covered mainten-ance of the tarmac roads, disposal of sewage and path-clearing during the winter.

BE A NOMAD

If you are not too weighed down by possessions, and enjoy a carefree or even nomadic existence, why not buy a boat? Many couples enjoy boat life and they can be extremely snug when fitted properly. The added advantage is you can get up and go to another area or another river bank almost whenever you choose. Many people prefer to live within a marina or boatyard that can offer limited facilities which will range from showers, a club house and even laundry facilities. Check with the local authority, water board or the marina for local by-laws. You may find you cannot live on the boat all the year round.

If you enjoy travelling around and not staying in any one place too long, it is possible to rent flats and houses in holiday areas during the winter months and then move out during the summer when they are rented out to holidaymakers.

LIVING IN

Have you considered becoming a cook/housekeeper or a chauffeur/handyman to someone who can afford to pay for such services? Good people are hard to find, and if you are willing to enter into the spirit of the venture and pull your weight, you won't find a shortage of jobs on offer. Don't forget though, that you will have to supply character references and persuade your future employer that you really can do the job, especially if you have had no previous experience.

SHELTERED HOUSING

You don't have to be a pensioner to consider sheltered hous-ing seriously. It may be that you want to throw off the drudgery of endless maintenance of your house and garden and at the same time look for somewhere smaller. You may be suffering from a disabling disease and feel you would like to move into purpose-built housing that recognises these limitations.

People from their mid-fifties onwards may seriously consider sheltered housing, and as builders have comparatively recently 'discovered' this gap in the market, it isn't difficult to find.

Initially, prices may seem high compared to the straight purchase price of other housing, but sheltered housing has some built-in extras to offer as well as built-in extra costs.

There is a complete range of accommodation on offer, from apartments in refurbished manor houses, a wide variety of flats in both large and small communities to one- or two-bedroomed bungalows or houses.

The development should offer the following advantages:

* A warden or secretary who can keep an eye on residents and summon help if needed.
* Some kind of community facilities – residents' lounge, laundry, for instance, or a guest bedroom that can be rented when you have visitors.
* Someone to be responsible for the maintenance of the property including decorating, window-cleaning and gardening.
* An alarm system.
* A high level of insulation to cut fuel costs. There should be relatively few stairs and in the case of flats, a lift. You may require waist-high electric plugs to avoid bending.

Other desirable attributes will be more a question of personal needs.

Many complexes are built within the centre of a town so that there is easy access to shops, the post office, banks and forms of recreation. The more isolated ones should at least be near some shops or pubs.

You may find public transport increasingly important to you as you get older, and even if you have a car, it is still sensible to be close to buses or a railway station.

There is no set pattern for these complexes. Each one is

different, and you should visit as many sites as you can to get the feel of them. You cannot guarantee any of the facilities described, but you can and must ask questions and get satisfactory answers about these and many other considerations.

If you are buying into an existing community, it is comparatively easy to ask other residents what they think, and to get the overall feel of the place. Does everyone seem contented or is there an endless list of complaints? What do they think about service charges and how is the maintenance of the property dealt with?

The service charge will almost certainly seem high because of the range of services involved, but you should satisfy yourself that the money is well spent and check if there is any limitation on the annual increases.

You may have to pay ground rent and this can vary greatly, so do check.

The warden or secretary plays a key role in any management scheme. The warden is really more of a good neighbour than a nurse, so she will not be able to help with getting you up or bringing you meals or doing any shopping. She will be able to contact relatives for you if necessary and help in the case of any emergency. She will sort out maintenance or repair problems and keep an eye on any communal facilities. In most schemes the warden will be on call at regular times, but this may not be 24 hours a day, so ask what happens when she is not available.

It is vital to take legal advice on the lease and any special points, such as buy-back arrangements, should you wish to move. It is normal for the management to have some control on your resale, and you will almost certainly have to sell it to an older person, but in some cases you may be asked to sell back at the price you paid, which cannot be good news for you considering the annual increase in housing prices. Don't sign anything without getting expert advice and make sure you understand everything in the document.

Age Concern publishes a booklet, *A Buyer's Guide to Sheltered Housing* which goes into the complex business in some detail. Ring the *New Homes Marketing Board* on its hotline, and ask for its free list of sheltered housing in appropriate areas and at suitable prices providing of course you are considering a brand new home.

LIVING ABROAD

Although, without doubt, there are very many couples who have made the break from Britain and are now living happily abroad in the sunshine, there appear to be large numbers who feel they have made a grave mistake.

It is incredible that anyone can part with life savings for a place in the sun without investigating every conceivable snag and possibility of what could go wrong.

When you consider the stress of moving house in this country, then add on the compound difficulties of language, different property laws and a sprinkling of people only too willing to part you from your hard-earned cash, it must be obvious that you should proceed with the greatest caution.

You must satisfy yourself that the person selling the property has the legal right to sell. Engage a local lawyer who can speak English, and make sure you understand everything in detail before you sign. Don't buy properties without viewing them first. Where possible, speak to other villa owners nearby and learn from them. Discuss any management charges or other on-going costs, and make sure you can afford it. If you are considering buying a business, it is even more important to investigate all angles of the transaction, including your obligations once you own it. Although it sounds harsh, don't take anything on trust – be satisfied in your own mind that everything is legally above-board.

Without my wishing to be a wet blanket, it has to be said that that is only half the story. Once you are installed in your villa, and have a suntan that most of your friends back home would envy, what do you do with the rest of your life? Many couples expect to live in a foreign country without even learning the language, so obviously their social life will be limited to other ex-patriates. It will be difficult to integrate with the local community even if you can speak the language and downright impossible if you cannot.

It is possible to make such a dramatic change of lifestyle and be happy, but the odds are stacked against it, so go carefully. Consider spending two or three months in the place as a long-stay holidaymaker (see page 169) before you get committed to something you may regret.

ADDRESS LIST

Age Concern, Bernard Sunley House, 60 Pitcairn Road, Mitcham, Surrey CR4 3LL. 01 640 5431

New Homes Marketing Board, 82 New Cavendish Street, London W1M 8AD. 01 935 7464

6
GOOD HEALTH

Whether you plan to go on working until you drop or whether you hope to finish work early in order to do other things, you will enjoy everything very much more if you can stay fit.

Being healthy is not, as people tended to think years ago, just a matter of not being ill. Most of us these days expect to enjoy positive health well into our later years. Positive health means having the dexterity, vitality and stamina to follow our chosen lifestyle and leisure pursuits. Positive health means having the energy to enjoy life to the full and not to be constantly suffering aches and pains or held back by a permanent feeling of tiredness.

How we feel is very largely in our own hands. It is true that our genes may have set the parameters and there is not a thing we can do about that. But that said, we can follow accepted medical guidelines and enjoy sensible eating and exercise patterns that will carry us through.

1. Keep an eye on your weight and avoid getting more than half a stone under or over your recommended range for your height.

2. Don't smoke.

3. Drink in moderation only.

4. Eat a varied diet but be moderate in your fat and sugar intake and try to cut down on salt.

5. Take regular exercise not only to increase stamina and strength but to maintain flexibility in joints.

6. Avoid undue stress.

Take a straight line across from your height (without shoes) and a line up from your weight (without clothes). Put a mark where the two lines meet.

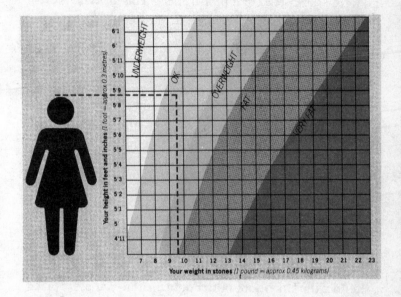

This chart, reproduced with the kind permission of the Health Education Authority, shows the desirable range of weight for your particular height. It is sensible to keep within those guidelines. Weigh yourself once a week at the same time of day. If you plan to undertake a strenuous course of dieting, it is advisable to check first with your doctor.

SENSIBLE EATING

It is important to eat well and regularly if you are to maintain your health.

Most people realise that as they get older they need fewer calories, and the tendency is to eat sketchily or have a diet of minor snacks instead of a proper meal. This attitude is often more entrenched if you live alone. It is easy to feel you cannot be bothered to get a meal for yourself and for the odd evening, or even longer, it doesn't matter too much. But if your regular diet becomes a slice or two of toast or a few biscuits instead of something more nourishing, you will certainly feel less lively and have less stamina to fight off minor coughs and colds or to combat a period of stress or extra tiredness.

Once again, it is getting into good habits that pays dividends. As you can gradually change your diet so that you rely less on cakes and biscuits as a top-up, so you can get used to preparing quick but nourishing meals for yourself.

Your daily needs are basically to drink, in some form or another half a pint of (preferably) skimmed milk, and to eat one portion of one of the following foods: lean meat, fish, poultry without the skin, eggs, cheese or pulses such as beans and lentils.

Restrict the amount of butter or margarine you use. Spread the fat as thinly as you can over your bread. If you are having bread with cheese, for example, you don't need any fat at all. Similarly if you are eating a coleslaw sandwich or any other moist filling, try going without the fat. Avoid fried or any generally fatty food unless you can trim it.

You can eat an almost unlimited quantity of vegetables, so it's worth experimenting to find out which kinds you can really enjoy rather than tolerate. Don't overcook them, as they will taste so much better if they are barely cooked, and a lot of vegetables taste marvellous raw. Eat potatoes with their skins on – the skin is a valuable source of fibre.

Eat at least one piece of fruit daily and include some kind of citrus fruit such as orange or grapefruit regularly. If you are still trying to wean yourself off reaching for the biscuit tin throughout the day, a piece of fruit such as a segment of orange or a few grapes will help.

Avoid eating too many sweets or starchy snacks. It is far better to eat three or even four small meals a day that are specially planned than to dispel hunger pangs with packets of crisps.

Food for Strong Bones

Calcium is necessary for strong bones. As we get older there is a tendency for bones to become more brittle, so make sure you eat enough foods containing calcium. These include milk, cheese (low fat varieties are available in both), nuts, yogurt and greens.

Protein Foods

Proteins are needed in our diet for body-building and repair. They are found in lean meat, fish, cheese, eggs, milk and pulse vegetables.

Foods Containing Iron

Liver and kidneys are both good sources of iron and so is red meat. Iron is also found in egg yolks and green vegetables.

Foods for Fibre

The case for increasing our fibre intake has been preached almost to death over the last few years. However, there is no doubt that we should all eat more than we do. It helps to prevent constipation and other diseases such as diverticulitis. Eat wholemeal bread, wholegrain breakfast cereals, pulses including baked beans, the skins of potatoes and plenty of green vegetables.

When you see what a variety of nourishing food there is to choose from, it's amazing how we still hanker for the less good sweet varieties. It is certainly wise to cut down on sugary foods, and that includes the less obvious ones such as some soft drinks and beer, but it is unrealistic to think that you will never eat or drink them again. If you can restrict your chocolate eating, for example, to one or two portions a week and to substitute fruit for sweet puddings and desserts except for weekends or when you have visitors, you will have gone a long way along the road to sensible eating.

DIETING

As far as losing weight is concerned, where possible tackle the extra pound or two before it becomes four or five and gets to be a major undertaking. Weigh yourself regularly, about once a week, always at the same time of day, in the nude if possible or wearing the same clothes.

There is no point in going on drastic diets, as the only way to lose pounds and then maintain your weight loss is to revise your eating patterns. If you have a severe weight problem – you need to lose a stone or more – consider joining one of the slimming clubs. These involve group therapy and you have a chance to join with others who are struggling too. The leaders are usually well-informed and can help a great deal with advice and diet sheets to suit you personally. Before you join, however, you must show that you are really committed to losing weight and not just playing at it.

The more you learn about the foods you eat, the more they will surprise you. It's not just cakes and pastries that can clock up the calories – they are hidden in butter and margarine, salad dressings and some flavoured yogurts as well as pickles and jams.

Even if you don't attend a slimming club, find out what causes your own particular calorie pile-up. Get to know exactly what it is that adds the pounds on you. Learn to recognise what a two-ounce slice of bread looks like and how big a bunch eight ounces of grapes is likely to be. It's a good idea to weigh everything for a time to see how much you eat. The knowledge may surprise you.

Keep an accurate note of what you eat and drink over a

couple of weeks, so that you can see what your current established eating patterns bring forth. Many people, for example, can quite happily trim their intake during the week but splash out more over the weekend. Within limits, i.e. that you don't blue your whole strategy in a Saturday night binge every week, you can find it easier to change your pattern within acceptable sociable limits.

You will find that over a period, you can stop loving rich Danish pastries and chocolate biscuits and prefer fruit. When you have that uncontrollable urge to eat a plateful of cake, you can gradually switch to low-calorie crispbread or a piece of celery. Try to find a substitute that you can enjoy. If eating a raw carrot instead of a bar of chocolate makes you cringe, you will never really forgo the habit.

Get used to substituting mineral water for soft drinks as well as alcoholic ones. A sparkling mineral water served with ice and lemon is a very acceptable pre-dinner drink. Soda water mixed 50/50 with dry white wine will halve the calories at a stroke. Avoid sweetened drinks as far as possible – diet drinks are fine up to a point, but then you will still enjoy the sweet taste instead of finding you can come to accept something else.

DRINK

Most people like the occasional tipple, and the medical profession in general agrees that it is good for people to drink in moderation, albeit not in conjunction with driving.

The Health Education Authority suggests that moderate drinking is defined as two to three pints of beer, or their equivalent, two to three times a week for men. For women, their guide is two to three standard drinks two to three times a week, but in this case, a standard drink would be half a pint of lager or a single pub measure of spirit or a glass of wine. Some recent opinion suggests these guidelines should be even lower.

The aim in having a sociable drink should be to help you unwind without it becoming habit-forming. Don't forget that even one drink can affect your judgement, and if you drank your 'quota' at one go it would most certainly do so.

On average, it will take an hour for your body to get rid of the alcohol in one standard drink, but longer if you are below average weight. If you are tired and hungry you will be affected more quickly too.

EXERCISE

When you consider the benefits of regular exercise, it seems quite astonishing that there is anyone left who doesn't participate in some form, but according to statistics there is still an army of armchair sportsmen and women who take no regular exercise at all.

Apart from being great fun, providing you choose a form you can enjoy and it is suitable for your overall condition, exercise will make you feel more energetic. It helps you relax and feel good; it can help you get slim and stay slim and keeps you supple. Some forms of sport can increase your stamina and help make your heart work more efficiently. In many cases it can relieve tension, although competitive people can sometimes get agitated when they don't win!

Fitness is generally defined by the three S factors – suppleness, strength and stamina. They are all important, and some activities are more useful than others in achieving the goals, though few will be significant in all three categories. Normally you will have to combine two or three.

* Suppleness keeps you mobile so that you can get in and out of cars and trains easily and stretch to do awkward jobs around the house or garden.
* Stamina enables you go keep going when tackling energetic jobs such as gardening or decorating and, of course, you need it if you are in a hurry to catch a bus.
* Strength is essential in lifting, carrying heavy objects or moving the furniture around.

If you plan to start taking exercise, it is essential to do it gently at first and build up gradually.

Always warm up first with a few bends and stretches and cool down afterwards. Most injuries are caused by going at exercise over-enthusiastically without taking the time to build up gradually over the first few weeks.

If you are not sure how you want to get moving, just content yourself by walking more and using your body in daily activities such as bending and stretching around the house or in the garden. You can build up quite a lot of extra activity by walking to the shops or past your regular bus stop on to the next. You can walk to a new fare stage and save money at the same time.

When you choose an activity, go for one you can really enjoy. It's no good taking up swimming if you hate feeling cold, or taking up a sport that involves team work if you prefer to be on your own.

Thankfully there is such a wide range to choose from that you can never use the excuse that you can't find one you would enjoy. The first stop is to find your local sports centre or swimming-pool to see what they have to offer. You will find your local library can help you, and many have a wide range of notices for would-be sports fans inviting you along to a local club, be it tennis, badminton or squash.

The Leisure or Recreation Department of your local authority will be able to tell you what is available in your area too, and you can see what's on by reading your local paper.

In your area you will almost certainly find a wide range of sports to tempt you. The more popular and simple ones mentioned here are easily available.

Swimming

Often quoted as the best all round sport to increase suppleness, stamina and strength. It will trim your figure and is marvellous if you have any stiffness, as the water supports you while you exercise. Swimming can be boring if you go with the single aim of doing so many lengths. Try to go with friends or your family. It is inexpensive. Find out at which times the pool is at its emptiest – you may not want to mix with the local school swimming lessons.

Cycling

Provides an extra bonus of being a cheap way to travel. It is good for stamina and helps to keep you moving. You can cycle on your own or join a group. Although new bikes are fairly expensive, you can get good second-hand ones. If you cycle at night wear reflective clothing. It is essential to keep your bike in good condition and observe the traffic codes.

Skipping

Nothing could be easier than buying a length of rope from your hardware store and skipping in the garden. It is good for stamina and useful in trimming your tummy. Don't overdo it at the beginning and stop if your knees or ankles hurt. Wear training shoes or those that give good support to feet and ankles.

Dancing

Strength, stamina and suppleness are all helped by dancing, and there is a tremendous variety of styles to choose from. Dancing classes are available in most towns. Adult Education classes will be cheaper than private ones. While learning, wear easy-fitting clothes and well-fitting shoes. You don't have to go as a couple, and the exercise can be as gentle or as strenuous as you wish.

Jogging

A popular sport at the moment that is good for stamina. Don't overdo it at first and run on soft surfaces like grass if you can. If you are overweight or have back, knee or ankle problems, it is probably better to try another sport. Otherwise you need a good pair of running shoes and comfortable clothing.

Bowling

It improves flexibility in shoulders and arms, and you are involved in bending and stretching. Bowls has a great social atmosphere, and you can play it in many parks, although there are now some indoor rinks. You will need flat shoes, and some clubs have rules about dress.

Exercise Classes and Yoga

Although these seem to be women-oriented, there is no reason why men cannot join in too. Yoga is excellent for suppleness. Exercise classes vary widely – some are pretty energetic and some cater especially for over 60s. There is usually a good choice via your local Adult Education Authority. You need comfortable clothing so many women wear leotards and footless tights.

FOOT CARE

It is difficult to be active when your feet hurt. The agony will show on your face too. It can make shopping trips and other outings a miserable affair instead of fun.

Look after your feet and they will reward you well. Practise foot exercises (see below) regularly.

Wear well-fitting shoes, and if you wear high heels, vary the heel size regularly. Don't get into the habit of wearing non-supportive slippers for long periods. Feet often get broader as you get older, so check the size you need from time to time and seek the advice of a trained shop assistant who can measure your feet.

It's not only shoes that need to fit well. Ill-fitting socks or tights can hamper foot movement as well. Don't let anything you wear on your feet restrict toe movement.

Keep your feet in good order by washing them every day in warm water without soaking. Dry them carefully, especially in between the toes. Sprinkle a little talcum powder in between the crevices.

Get used to walking about barefoot around the house as it will stengthen the muscles and harden the skin. Keep a look-out for patchy redness, especially between the toes – it could be athlete's foot. Ask your chemist for some special foot powder or seek the advice of a chiropodist.

Keep toenails short and cut them straight across either with clippers or sharp nail scissors or a nail file.

Corns or other callouses should really be seen by a chiropodist, as should any other foot problems.

Sweating feet can be washed in lukewarm water and dried

carefully. Try to go barefoot as much as you can and wear natural fibre shoes and socks.

If you have to stand all day, vary the height of your shoes throughout the period.

Foot Exercises

When you are sitting down, cross your legs and rotate each ankle clockwise and anti-clockwise.

With bare feet pick up a pencil with your toes. Repeat ten times daily.

Always take the opportunity to sit with your feet up when you can.

EYES

Our vision changes as we get older, and most of us resort to spectacles when we find it increasingly difficult to read except at arm's length.

It is important to have your eyes tested every two years, more frequently if you suspect that anything may be wrong.

You will find that you see less well in the dark, and it takes the eye longer to refocus when you move from a well-lit area into a darker one. This could affect your driving, so extra care should be taken. The quality of light by which you read or do any job around the house will become increasingly important, otherwise you will suffer from eye fatigue.

Work in a good light. If you cannot work in daylight, have a good clear bulb focused over your left shoulder so that the pool of light falls on your work. If your eyes tire, rest them. Cupping the eyes can help and so can lying down with eye-pads – cotton wool soaked in cold water or witch-hazel.

If limited vision is your problem, you will, of course, be receiving expert advice. Your consultant will be able to give you specific instructions for your problems. You will need to do as much as you can to get the right amount of light when undertaking various tasks. In some cases, with cataracts for instance, you may need less light not more.

As a general rule, you will need sufficient light where it is needed, without glare. It is important not to have too much variance in light levels – reading under a pool of light in an otherwise darkened room should be avoided. You should also avoid a substantial difference between light levels in different rooms as it will take the eye some time to adjust to the change.

Make the most of daylight by positioning furniture so that you can take advantage of the light rather than have it obscured. Keep room decorations light and bright, and clean windows will obviously allow in more light than dirty ones.

Artificial light is not harmful to the eyes, but if you don't get the source of light in the right position, you can strain your eyes and this can lead to headaches.

Avoid working in a shadow and don't choose inadequately shielded lights – a bare bulb, for instance, is not a good idea.

EARS

You may experience some loss of hearing in later life, and it is most likely the high-pitch sounds that go. It may mean that you cannot hear some of the newer telephone rings or that you cannot tune into a conversation if there is a lot of background noise.

If the inconvenience is more than minimal, have a word with your doctor. The trouble may be caused by wax in the ear which he can syringe for you. Don't be tempted to poke around in your own ear – it is extremely delicate and you could cause damage.

If there is no obvious cause, your doctor may refer you to an ear, nose and throat specialist.

TEETH AND GUMS

If you have taken care of your teeth and avoided eating too many sugary foods and visited your dentist regularly, you should find your teeth in reasonable condition. What happens in later life is that our gums recede, and you should check this regularly with your dentist.

Visits to the dentist should be every six months or at more frequent intervals if you have any problems. He can file down sharp edges of teeth that can cause discomfort and check that harmful plaque is not present as well as giving your teeth and gums a routine examination.

STRESS

Stress is not a bad thing in itself. The reaction to challenge can offset boredom and make you work at your peak. It can help you think clearly and gear you up to physical demands. We all react differently to the amounts of stress in our lives, and some are certainly better-equipped to deal with it than others.

When we endure too much stress, we are at risk, as it can be linked to heart disease, high blood pressure, peptic ulcers and arthritis.

Once you realise that you are under stress, for whatever reason, take positive steps to ease it. Physical activity is one of the best ways, which is why so many high-powered executives – fit ones – take up squash. You may find release in going for a jog or doing some vigorous work around the house. If you practise yoga or meditation, you will have learned specific techniques that allow you to unwind.

Don't resort to tranquillisers or cigarettes to calm you down. Learn to deal with the difficulty by facing up to the root cause and finding your own best evasive action.

SLEEP

We generally need less sleep as we get older, but any one person's pattern can vary so much from another throughout life that there is no set of guidelines as to how much we will need.

It is important to have enough sleep to charge our batteries and restore our energy, but this can vary between four or five hours and eight or nine.

Sufficient sleep is a certain a way of looking your best and keeping mentally alert. If you find you can't sleep at night, you may discover that you can catnap during the day. That short nap after lunch can be extremely regenerative and give you added impetus for the late afternoon and evening.

Lying awake at night fretting that you can't sleep is to be avoided. Get up, make a warm drink or give up thoughts of sleep altogether and read a book or do some simple jobs that you meant to do during the day.

Solutions to problems you have solved at night very often don't bear daytime scrutiny, so avoid making any major decisions during these night-time sessions. The yoga technique of positively relaxing every part of your body, starting from your toes and working upward, very often works and so, surprisingly, can counting sheep!

To start in the best frame of mind for a good night's sleep, avoid tea, coffee or other stimulants from early evening onwards. If you like a drink before retiring, make it a milky one.

Take a warm bath before you go to bed.

Avoid stimulating or upsetting books or television programmes in the last hours before bedtime. Aim to unwind and do something quiet and relaxing instead. Taking the dog for a walk is one suggestion.

Make sure your bedroom is warm but not hot. Check that your mattress is comfortable. Don't be kept awake by dripping taps or banging doors – if neighbours are noisy, consider earplugs.

7
LOOKING GOOD

The way you look is going to influence the way people feel about you, and even more important, the way you feel about yourself. No-one can put back the clock, and all of us will have to recognise that we look older as the years pass by. It isn't necessary to feel dispirited about it or ever think it is not worth the time and effort required to keep fit and look our best.

Even when our relationships have reached zero, or we feel bereft of companions, or particularly low after an illness, we should, and indeed most will, want to make some effort to look attractive.

It is important psychologically to make an effort for your own sake, even if for nothing else. Sometimes after a severe illness, the first sign of getting better is for patients to want to wash their hair, or for a woman to want to put on some make-up.

Looking good isn't just a case of keeping trim, with well-cut hair and as good a skin as one can manage. It is in posture, the way we walk and how we approach people, that reveals our attitude to life and what is going on around us. How often have you looked in the mirror one morning and said a mental, 'Ugh!', yet on other mornings, 'Not so bad, there's still some life in me yet.'

It is important to maintain good posture and a spring in your step. One of the first things that actors learn is how to move in a 'heavy' way to convey age, so avoid that mistake as far as you can. It is particularly obvious when you sit down and stand up. Watch how young people move, then compare your own gait and decide what can be done to improve matters.

Some people look 70 in their forties, yet others can still betray an enthusiasm for life in their eighties, which reveals itself in an interested manner and permanent sparkle in the eye.

Being involved in what goes on around us is important at any age, yet even more so when we are more on the sidelines and less involved in the nitty-gritty. If you have a zest for life and an interest in what goes on, you will look lively and consequently younger. Isn't it infuriating, when attempting to start up a conversation with acquaintances of any age, to find they don't read the newspapers, seldom watch anything on television or play any form of sport? Their responses are negative – they claim they have no time for this or that because they have a family to care for, an elderly mother to wait upon or a demanding job.

Just because you have a demanding, and to you, interesting job, doesn't mean that you can't bore the pants off other people if it is your only interest. Being a whizz-kid in computers or a fount of information about the education system doesn't mean that you are interesting to others outside that sphere. It is so important to keep alive all sorts of interests even if you have to maintain them from an armchair instead of being in the thick of it.

Take on board the new technology – go on a computer course at evening class instead of saying you can't keep up with what is happening. Get a book out of the library on a famous musician or listen to tapes. Study German or do something outside your normal sphere. Read specialist magazines in a subject that you'd like to know more about, whether it is videos, sailing or ballroom dancing.

Keeping up interests ensures a spring in your step and an alert look in your eye which is always attractive, regardless of age.

GOOD GROOMING

'A sweet disorder in her dress,' as the poet said, may seem endearing at seventeen but is distinctly less so at any later age.

Good grooming and attention to details are essential in both men and women. For men it is equally important to keep their figures as far as they can and not to pretend that fat stomachs and bulging waistlines are cuddly. There is far less need these days to wear formal suits all the time, and it is easier to disguise figure faults with casual-style trousers, safari shirts or loose-fitting anoraks. Avoid stiff, inflexible fabrics and don't be afraid to choose brighter colours for casual wear.

Pay particular attention to hair, and don't postpone getting it trimmed. Keep hands and particularly fingernails well manicured.

It is a mistake for a man to go overboard to look younger than he is in terms of juvenile clothes or an excess of gold medallions or over-tight jeans. There is considerable attraction in looking (and being!) mature, as long as it is combined with fitness, no excess fat and an air of interest and zest for life.

For women the same attention to figure and grooming apply, but convention accepts that they can and should do more to disguise the passing years.

MAINLY FOR WOMEN

Your Hair

Your hair is a most important beauty asset – healthy shiny hair that moves is always attractive. As you get older it is important to rule out the heavy static styles that rely on hairspray to keep them in place at all costs. By all means use spray, and rollers to set hair if you wish, but use the aids more to give body not to make a sculpture.

Find a hairdresser who is prepared to take an interest in you, not one who treats you like something coming off a conveyor belt. A good stylist should be prepared to discuss with you a style and cut, bearing in mind the sort of life you lead and how skilled you are at caring for your own hair.

It is possible to shed years from your looks with a suitable hairstyle and colour. In general terms it is better to go lighter in colour as you mature. Lighter tones are generally softer, and remember lighter doesn't only mean blonde.

Go grey if you wish and if you think it suits you, otherwise be guided by a good hairdresser at least in the first instance. Don't attempt to colour your hair at home until you have established a suitable shade, and even then, if you do decide to tint at home, go for semi-permanent or shampoo-in colourants. Another tip if you wish to colour hair at home is not to alter the shade dramatically, just make small changes.

Grey hair can look attractive, but I cannot honestly say I have ever met anyone who looked younger with such colouring. If you want to stick to grey, keep your hair in tip-top condition and consider giving it a rinse in a silver tone to avoid the yellow look, or streak with white to give the hair a lift.

You may find it is better to avoid severe styles, such as hair scraped back and heavy geometric cuts. A softer look can disguise a double chin or a prominent nose. A wispy fringe will hide frown lines.

By now you will know what style suits you generally, but do stand back and take a long careful look at yourself at regular intervals. Hairstyles that flattered in your twenties may look very dated. If you have put on weight, especially if you have plumped out around the jawline, you may need to take stock and choose a new style.

Soft curls on the crown with a soft frame around the ears is generally a flattering style for most people. Too much curl is aging and so can be a positive mane of hair.

Get ideas from public figures you admire who still look up to date and positively glamorous, though not in the first flush of youth. Even if their face shapes are different from yours, a good stylist will explain how you can adapt a style to suit your own bone structure or, if the cut relies on thick heavy hair when yours is fine and sparse, he will point out that you will only be disappointed with the results.

A heavy jawline can be disguised by giving width at the temples and above the ears. Avoid fullness of hair elongating your jawline. If your hair finishes at your jaw it will extend the line and draw attention to the area.

A double chin recedes if you have hair away from chin level and ears. Curls massed on the crown and upswept hair in a soft style can look attractive too, and the same styles will suit anyone with a short, thick neck.

Don't have hair too long or too short – avoid extremes and remember that softer is better, in terms of both colour and style. Look at your hair in conjunction with your whole figure – don't just look in a mirror at head and shoulders, but judge the whole effect by looking at yourself full length. Then you can see that the proportions of hair and face to body are sympathetic.

Another way of giving hair a lift is to have 'sun streaks' bleached or painted in. The sun streaks that are bleached in are better done professionally, but some highlights can be done quite simply at home. As always it is essential to follow the manufacturer's instructions very carefully and take a patch test first.

Skin Care

By the time you reach middle years, the routine of skin care that you have carried out since your teens will determine how you look. Regular sensible skin care from an early age gives abundant benefits later on.

Undoubtedly, you will have established some kind of routine, but it is possible to keep on with the one you have had for years without taking note of the new products and improvements that have taken place in the meantime.

Cleansing, toning and nourishing are still the same vital words, and how you cleanse your face is really a matter of preference, so there is no point in adding to the controversy over soap and water or cleansing creams.

The particular things you will notice as you get older are that your skin gradually gets a more mottled appearance and it will gradually begin to feel drier. Lines and wrinkles will appear too.

There is no point in pretending that all this can be avoided, and it would be a thankless task to even try to eliminate them all.

Smoking produces extra lines that you can do without, and certain facial expressions add their share as well.

One thing that becomes increasingly important is to slough off the dead scales of skin. The use of a loofah on the body is a great bonus, particularly if you smooth in body lotion after you have towel-dried. Use a facial scrub on the face and neck, avoiding under the eyes and around the mouth. Follow the manufacturer's instructions and don't use it more than once a week.

A pumice stone is still helpful, though rather harsh, but is great for hard skin on the feet and elbows. Use it wet and keep at it little and often to remove hard skin on the soles of the feet, for example.

Moisturiser should always be used on the face. Don't feel you only need it once a day. Put it on frequently if you aren't using any other make-up, and, for example, it is essential before you go out in a drying wind.

You should have been using a specially formulated eye-cream since your early twenties, but if you haven't, start now. There are plenty to choose from. Many of the more expensive ones come in trial sample packs, so take advantage of that. Vaseline can be used very gently, fingerprinted under the eye area, but it is rather heavy to use regularly although gloriously inexpensive. Use it on the lips too if they feel dry or chapped.

Once you reach a certain age – and you will know when better than anyone – there is no doubt that women look better with a little make-up. You won't find many famous older stars even popping out to post a letter without wearing some. A light foundation cream over moisturiser evens out skin tone and blusher works wonders especially when you are feeling tired. Also by making the effort you will feel better in yourself and the results will speak for themselves.

Make-up

Good make-up in mid and later years means less not more. Nothing is going to cover lines and wrinkles, but a discreet colouring can give you a sparkle when one is lacking.

If you can, visit a beauty salon from time to time to find out the current make-up trends. Eye make-up techniques and the choice of colours change regularly, sometimes quite dramatically. It's easy to put years on without realising it by using out of date make-up techniques.

If you can't find a salon or don't want to have a treatment or a make-up lesson, look at the magazines. The weeklies in particular show up-to-date make-up techniques quite regularly.

Don't, in your quest to keep up to date, follow fashions that plainly don't suit you. Your aim should be to look healthy and glowing by using subtle shades that flatter your own colouring.

Don't try to change your basic skin tone. Ask the shop assistant's advice but choose a time when she isn't too busy. The counters in department stores are better for advice than busy chemist shops.

No-one can halt the passage of time, and in our hearts, not that many of us want to. The thought of a 50-year-old with no laughter lines is almost unseemly. What we can do, however, is make the most of our assets – this is good sense in all facets of life, whether in high finance or in our appearance.

Whether you wear make-up every day or only occasionally is a personal choice. There's the school of thought that advises us to give our skins a rest to allow it to breathe, but it is always on the day you meet a friend you haven't seen for years or an ex-boyfriend.

Most women can't look their best without the helping hand of a good moisturiser – good being identified as the one that suits her own skin the best – and a light foundation to even out the skin tone. Blusher nearly always improves the situation as long as you don't overdo it.

To disguise certain bad points there are some tricks of the trade.

1. Double chin, heavy jaw line
Use a darker foundation in an elongated triangle just above the weighty part, i.e. jowls. Blend into your normal foundation along the edges then set with transluscent powder.

2. Drooping eye lids
Take your eye-liner pencil and start with a thin line at the inner corner of your upper lid and widen it progressively until it covers the outer corner. Then 'fudge' the line with your normal eye-shadow.

3. Dark circles under the eye
Use a concealer-stick one or two shades lighter than the skin tone. Fingerprint to blend gently, then use normal foundation.
4. Deep-set eyes
Line the outer halves of the upper lid with a darkish eyeline pencil, widening the line as you approach the outer edge. Apply normal shadow over it and smudge it over to blur the line. Deep-set eyes can also be 'brought forward' by dotting a light pink or pale cream in the centre of the top eye lid and blending it in to your other eye colour.
5. Broad nose
To make a nose narrower, draw triangles of foundation two or three shades darker than your normal foundation on either side of the bone. Blend into the surrounding normal foundation.
6. Indistinct lip shape
Lip colour that 'bleeds' around the edges can be set by out-lining your lips with a lip-pencil and then brushing lipstick inside the line. Lip-brushes are more effective than just using lipstick straight on to the lips. If you want to alter their shape, you can cheat by putting the outline to the outside or inside of your natural colour. Use a light textured lipstick, not frosted or too opaque. Keep to a light colour that still shows on your lips.
7. Vertical lines
A tip for minimising the lines from nose to lips is to stick your tongue behind your top lip so that it pushes out the skin when you blend in foundation. If you use loose powder, use the same technique and you'll find that the make-up doesn't set in the lines.

What You Wear

There is so much good advice about choosing clothes that applies to any age, but I think that some of it is extra important in the more mature years.

Know what suits you and stick to it. This includes foods that agree with you, colours that suit you and routines which are healthy and suit your lifestyle.

Don't be afraid to take time off to look at yourself in the

mirror. Consider your body naked full length and come to terms with what you see and determine to improve what offends you.

Undertake a lifelong beauty and exercise routine that will improve or at least maintain your appearance.

Take note of fashions but don't follow them slavishly. You should know your figure faults by now, so disguise what you can and be philosophical about what really cannot be altered. Avoid exposing too much flesh – especially upper arms and elbows. Learn to draw attention away from your bad points by emphasising the good.

Rediscover which colours suit you best and stick to them regardless of fashion, or at least make them the basic colours in your wardrobe. Remember that as your skin and hair tones change so will the shades that flatter.

Keep an eye on hemlines – they change regularly, and although there is much more of a range of acceptable hemlines these days, skirts and jackets can sometimes look very dated when, by altering the hemline they can be saved.

As far as you are able, develop a style. Be outrageous if you want, as long as you will really enjoy it and have the confidence to carry it off. Make the most of accessories – you can make scarves or bandeaux out of fabric oddments or buy them cheaply in chain-stores. Where you know that something will only last a season before it is old news, there's no point in spending too much.

Save your hard-earned cash for classics like skirts, blouses and jackets that can always look up to date by adding carefully chosen accessories.

Taking an interest in fashion and having the wisdom to adapt the trends to suit your own figure and lifestyle will pay dividends. The careful use of up-to-date accessories, the acceptance of new styles and fashion fabrics can subtly update how you look and, equally important, show to everyone that you are still in touch with the world.

Don't take up any trend that will make you feel uncomfortable – too high a heel, if you aren't used to them, tight belts, clinging fabrics over a wide bottom, for example.

Look for bright, not garish colours that you know will

flatter. Move from shades of white to cream, especially near the face. You can still wear classic styles but they will be more suitable in a bright shade rather than sombre or neutral shades. Avoid any colours that make you fade into the background – you will feel invisible, and if that sounds appealing to you, then it shouldn't! Pale tones will always enlarge, so beware!

Avoid stiff fabrics or masculine styles, and look for clothes that move. Now is the time to make the most of your femininity. If you have a good bustline, which should be midway between your shoulder and your elbow, be subtle, but draw attention to it and don't hide it under excessively baggy sweaters. If you have natty ankles, make sure your skirt line, shoes and tights will draw attention to them. Remember toning tights and shoes will make your legs look longer. Plain court shoes are the most universally flattering. When you have a trim waist, don't hide it.

Most of us have a rounded stomach at this stage in life, so wear skirts or trousers with gentle gathers at the waist or an A-line rather than something absolutely straight.

Long tunics can flatter if you have a bulging midriff or less than trim waist, though check that the tunic line ends below your buttocks rather than cutting in above them.

Buy a well-fitting bra, one that is the right size and doesn't leave folds of flesh bulging over.

Most of us have ample bottoms, so disguise the fact with longer shirt-style blouses or sweaters, or trousers and skirts that are loose over the largest areas. Avoid clinging fabrics. Flat yokes that flare out over the hips may accentuate your shape unfavourably as well.

Keep an eye on fashion magazines to see what the trend-setters are wearing. Sometimes an existing outfit topped with a shirt or a long waistcoat will transform it into this year's style. A belt worn at the hip instead of tightly round the waist, or a scarf twisted and knotted around your head will bring you up to date at no extra expense. Don't be afraid to experiment, but beware of asking your immediate family what they think – they will usually tell you the truth, but as they see it and not necessarily as viewed by the rest of the world.

8

MANAGING YOUR MONEY

This chapter on finance is written with the assistance of John Burke, founder of *The Stockbroker* and financial editor of *50 Plus* and associate editor of *What Investment?*

Finance is fearsome for many people, especially when means are limited. Still, those expecting a large lump sum (from retirement, redundancy or a maturing insurance policy, inheritance etc.) may well feel that life begins at 40 plus.

However, even a nest egg will not last for ever, and in the end, the financial situation must be faced. On one hand, savings and other assets must be invested wisely so as to maximise income in line with safety and your future requirements. On the other, you must plan to live within the income you get from this and other sources such as part-time work, pensions and any other government allowances.

This takes skilful planning, even for those who are good at arithmetic or economics, let alone investment. There are, however, five what might be called ground-rules to help:

1. Accept change as inevitable

We live at a time of faster change than that experienced by any previous generation, largely because scientific developments are making the global economy more complicated. The lesson to be learned is to be as nimble and adaptable as possible in matters of money. Obviously, if you have a basic pension and little else, your flexibility will be almost nil, but if you have money to invest, you must be alert to changes that will affect you, take advantage of what is good and try to minimise what is bad. In any case, endeavour to hedge your bets when planning for the future.

2. Know your objectives

It is also important to be clear about your aim with your finances. You should ensure that these aims fit in with other factors. For example, are you likely to move house (which is discussed more fully in Chapter 5) and what effect will this have on your requirements? There is no perfect plan for investing £50,000 or whatever, and in any case, no two individuals will have exactly the same circumstances. So anyone about to take out a self-employed pension may choose different terms if no dependants are involved from someone with dependants, and this might even affect the choice of insurance company. A more obvious example is deciding whether to stay on in a family-sized home in familiar surroundings or to move to something smaller in a cheaper area, thus making a cash profit.

3. Consider Taxation

In any matter of investment, it is essential to look at the effects of taxation. On retirement one's tax band can alter with changes to liability for higher rates of income-tax. This could dictate a change of investment strategy. Capital gains tax does not normally affect lower- to moderate-income groups. Those with heirs and sizeable assets, including the home they own, might want to look at schemes for reducing inheritance tax (previously called death duty or capital transfer tax).

4. Allow for getting older

It should be borne in mind the fact that getting older affects not only the premiums for life insurance, but also whether to opt for an annuity (see page 139).

It is sensible to prepare early, financially speaking, for future waning powers of the eyes, limbs and mind. For a start, the bank and branch you prefer now may prove to be not as convenient to you in ten or 25 years time. Apart from ease of access, there is also the question of dealing with paperwork. Investments, spread all over the place, may be good for spreading risks but may involve more work which older people find a nuisance.

5. Take advice

Unless your means and needs are small and simple, it will be hard to take the right investment decisions without advice. You can get the answer to some basic, straightforward questions from reading the financial pages in newspapers and magazines or even from the DHSS etc. But you may want to consult someone like your bank manager.

The problem is that there is no such thing as a perfect financial adviser. Nobody knows it all and, even more important, nobody does anything for nothing. There are many vested interests on hand to sell you all sorts of services from life assurance to deposits in building societies, and when you consider their commission can range up to nearly 100 per cent of your first premium, you can see it cannot be unbiased advice.

There are two ways to help in getting the advice best suited to your circumstances and ensuring that you are covered against greed, incompetence or dishonesty. In the first place, ask for rival alternative opinions, preferably from people specialising in different fields. For example, a bank manager may well have a view favourable to investment in or through the bank whereas an insurance broker will opt for some form of insurance. Neither will be expert in the other's field. A solicitor should declare if he gets a commission through you but he will charge you for his advice. He could well spot legal loopholes or problems which an accountant might miss.

With the increased complexity of financial services, unless you are one of the fortunate few who can afford to buy really independent advice, perhaps the best advice can be gained from a knowledgeable friend.

Secondly, always check the credentials of financial intermediaries who must now be licensed or have a recognised professional qualification. Your bank manager should help. Don't be too impressed with lots of letters after anyone's name until you know exactly what they stand for.

Following the Financial Services Act 1986 there is now a three-tiered way of complaining right the way up to the *Securities and Investments Board* which can give up to £48,000 in compensation where the company has gone into liquidation and the investor has suffered loss as a result.

The system for dealing with grievances also includes ombudsmen for banking and insurance.

However, that is only as a last resort. You must aim to get the best possible advice early on to avoid situations which involve ombudsmen. If still in doubt, stick to safe places for your money such as National Savings or building societies.

BANKS, BUILDING, SOCIETIES, FRIENDLY SOCIETIES

If you have had a good relationship with your branch for some years, then stay with it in the hope that your loyalty will be noted if you go through a bad time. Banks now provide the widest range of financial services, ranging from arranging wills and setting up trusts to share-dealing and making safe-boxes available. Check on their charges for these services and compare them against the competition.

The banks also issue credit cards. Use them as widely as possible, for provided you look after them and they aren't stolen, they are safer than cash and save the trouble or expense of cheques. You must be disciplined and pay up by the due date, in which case they can provide up to seven weeks credit, otherwise the interest payments are considerable.

Almost all banks offer free banking to customers whose accounts remain in credit, so keep it like that, but do not allow large sums to remain idle. You may find it useful to have a budget account where you pay in a certain amount each month and pay bills as they become due. Sometimes your account may be overdrawn, at other times in credit. You will incur charges on this type of account but it is a good way of spreading the load. Make sure you know what the charges are before you start.

Most banks offer poor rates of interest for deposit accounts, which are taxed at source without refund, except in places like the Isle of Man or the Channel Islands. Several offer cheque accounts with high interest for a minimum deposit (HICA for short) but these rates tend to be below the best offered by building societies.

Much of what has been said about banks may also (and

increasingly) apply to building societies, although their main interest will always be to provide mortgages for home buyers and a good home for savings. In 1986 they were empowered to undertake many banking and other sevices such as giving consumer credit and issuing cheque books and travellers cheques. Remember that the larger the sum and the longer it is agreed to be left, the higher the interest is likely to be.

The various plans and varying rates of interest are far too complicated and sometimes verge on the obtuse. Check with the independent *Building Society Shop* in Nottingham or subscribe to *Building Society Choice*.

Most people in their forties will already have experienced getting a mortgage if they are ever going to, but in the event of requiring one, remember some societies have very different attitudes to such factors as age, sex, old houses and inner cities. A mortgage broker may be able to help you, but remember he will be receiving a commission both from the building society or bank and, if you take out insurance, from the insurance company too.

There are two limited means of improving on building societies' interest, which is normally paid net of tax and which cannot be reclaimed. Several societies have accounts paying gross interest to Britons abroad. There are friendly societies which can bump up the net rate through ten-year plans which include decreasing life assurance.

INSURANCE

Life assurance (payment on death) becomes complicated in one's forties. This is because the cost of cover is a curve linked to age and it becomes steeper towards the age of 50, after which the premiums are considerable.

The simplest insurance is 'whole life' whereby you pay premiums as long as you live, so the insurance company takes a gamble as to when it will pay up. 'Term assurance' is for a fixed number of years and could be good for covering school fees (financing them is a form of saving, rather than assurance in case you die). There is also 'convertible term' which allows flexibility about the length and type of assurance. Dearer than term is 'family income benefit', while dearest of all is 'endowment' although a 'with profits' policy is also quite a good way to save.

Unfortunately, almost all new assurance lost relief of tax (LAPR) in 1984, so avoid surrendering any policy taken out before then. If you are hard up, it is better to borrow than do that, and the older endowment policies include a clause offering cheap loans.

The exceptions are policies for expatriates and those with 10 per cent relief in the Isle of Man. Those in Britain which are linked to self-employed pensions get relief at the highest rate of income tax. If you work for yourself or are in a job without a pension, you qualify for tax relief on a pension scheme approved by the Inland Revenue. Contact an insurance broker. The tax benefits are so good that there can be an advantage in it even up to the one year before retirement, but it is best to start in your forties with an option to take the pension between 60 and 75.

Premiums can be single ones (on which the broker gets less commission) or regular ones each year. As the government is changing the whole scope of National Insurance and private pensions this year this is a further factor to consider when making an overall decision about contributions. At all events, work out the alternatives on paper, bearing in mind projected life expectancy of yourself and your spouse.

Life assurance companies offer yet one more form of pension, namely lump sum annuities. In this case you hand over a single premium to the company, which guarantees to pay a fixed amount each year until you die. If you go next year, they win, but you could live until 109! Usually these annuities are written for a fixed minimum term (five or ten years), and in the event of the life assured predeceasing that date, the balance, the amount due to the end of the fixed period, becomes immediately payable to the estate. In reality, the insurance company puts your money into government stocks which you could do yourself and keep the capital in your own hands. But after the age of 75, it might be better to go for an annuity for reasons of actuarial arithmetic.

Don't overlook the fact that you will need various other

kinds of insurance ranging from accident/disability and holiday to house and contents. The insurance industry – both life and non-life, delights in inventing brand-new schemes. Some are just gimmicks, but you may find a scheme tailor-made to your requirements, linking various types of cover. Shop around through a good insurance broker who should have it all on computer. Before you sign, take time to read and understand the policy, taking special note of the inevitable exclusion clauses.

THE STOCK MARKET

Investing directly or indirectly in stocks and shares has become increasingly popular since the late 1970s. The money men never tire of telling us that savings will do better on the *Stock Exchange*, because £100 in the building society remains £100 plus erratic interest whereas company dividends grow and grow – while the value of the shares themselves goes up and up. Fine until there is a setback – like those in 1974 and 1987.

Broadly speaking, a good spread of equities – ordinary shares – should perform better than money accumulating in the building society – in the long run. As you get older it is important to adopt an investment policy geared to rising income, which means dividends, rather than going for capital growth.

Generally you need at least £50,000 to get a good spread of say, £2,000 in 25 stocks. This makes dealing costs worthwhile and cuts the risk by spreading the load. If in doubt, go for safe stocks like bank and insurance companies. Never mind the overall market's level; buy each share when it is relatively low and sell only if it goes amazingly high. And remember, greed, panic and dabbling ruin good investment.

You will need a stockbroker, and the Stock Exchange has (among many free leaflets) a list of members who like private clients. There are also licensed dealers in high street locations who make their money by the difference between buying and selling prices. They may be simpler and cheaper, but at the moment these members of *FIMBRA* do not have a compensation scheme (unlike stock-brokers) should they go bust before they have paid you after selling shares for you.

Many stockbrokers will also manage your investments for a fee, if you care to sign over maybe £50,000 or more to their care. If it is on a discretionary basis, they take the decisions on what to buy and when to sell. There is also the administrative portfolio, in which you give the instructions and they do the paperwork. Lloyds Bank has a similar scheme for lump sums of £25,000 complete with a so-called cash sweep so that spare funds remain in your own bank account.

UNIT TRUSTS, INVESTMENT TRUSTS, CURRENCY FUNDS

The rules of risk and reward that apply to stocks and shares largely apply equally to unit trusts. However, there are at least three reasons why unit trusts are better for the small investor than investing in individual companies.

Firstly, each trust pools the money from its unit holders or subscribers and invests it over a spread of 50 or more companies, so that any fall in the share price of one of the companies will have little effect on the diminution of the investments collectively. Secondly, the managers deal with all the work and worry of buying and selling each stock in the trust – backed by research and technology which the individual investor lacks. Thirdly, units in the trust are bought straight from the managers without having to find a stockbroker and pay him commission plus VAT.

Admittedly there are fees involved in unit trusts – typically 5 per cent initially and then half a per cent to one and a half per cent each year (plus VAT). However, this is built into the price of the units through a spread between the offer price (at which you buy) and the bid price (at which you sell). This spread is usually around 6 per cent but can double under difficult conditions. Clearly, if you buy units standing at 100 pence they must rise by at least 6 pence before you start to make a profit.

Remember, however, that while the value of unit trusts can fall as well as rise, the performance of veterans like *M & G* has shown the overall trend is upwards. People reliant on investment for income should in any case be buying unit trusts for income that rises in the long term (as the dividends grow from each company in the trust) rather than for more speculative capital growth. So choose unit trusts with names like Income, Mixed Income or High Yield.

Apart from that, it is extremely difficult to point the way to the ideal unit trust, as their places in the charts vary each year like snakes and ladders. Slow but sure are the general trusts, whereas the specialised ones can boom some years and then go into the doldrums. Altogether there are over 1,000 unit trusts divided into fifteen categories which are based on the world's regions or stock exchange's sectors where they invest.

So the field is confusing even if you study the monthly or yearly league tables. But here are two (speculative) tips: managers of a stable of unit trusts tend to put undue effort into their newest creation; and some investors claim that the worst performer of one year should show a healthy recovery (thus a gain) next time.

Much the same might be said of investment trusts, which so often are confused with unit trusts. However there are at least three big differences. The 200 or so investment trusts are all quoted on the stock exchange, so you must normally go through a stockbroker.

Because investment trusts consist not of units but shares – their capital is fixed, so the size of the fund does not wax and wane like unit trusts where holders put in money, usually during a boom, and pull it out, often during a slump. For this and other reasons, including permission to borrow money, which unit trusts cannot do, investment trusts are more economically run and their performance can be better. Also, for complicated reasons, the price of an investment trust's share is usually below that of the value of the shares of the companies in which it has invested. This so-called discount makes for a higher dividend and thus greater income.

Finally, a third alternative to unit and investment trusts is currency funds. These are managed offshore, and they pool the monies received into a basket of currencies, deposited with foreign banks, with the aim of riding fluctuations. Also offshore, there are several unauthorised unit trusts – in other words not vetted by the Department of Trade. For more information contact the *Unit Trust Association* or the *Association of Investment Trust Companies*.

NATIONAL SAVINGS, POST OFFICE, GOVERNMENT BONDS

The supreme advantage of National Savings is that your money is absolutely safe, because it is backed by the state. The government guarantees the planned rates of interest and promises to pay back your original capital (even if it is out of what it gets from future borrowing and tax payments). The only risk of loss is that of getting lower interest than otherwise, due, for instance, to being in a five-year plan when inflation or market rates make the promised return relatively unattractive. That is why the government came out with index-linked savings such as the so-called Granny Bonds.

Another advantage of National Savings is their flexibility, for there seems to be a form of saving suitable for everyone – including the Premium Bonds for those prepared to gamble away the interest. The range of ten or so plans includes some which help both non-taxpayers and those who have to pay at higher rates. National Savings certificates (each issue has different interest) are tax free as is the Yearly Plan for monthly savings. Taxable, but with interest paid gross, are Income and Deposit Bonds which pay the highest rates.

If you pay tax at standard rate, National Savings rarely offer more than the best of the building societies. So first look at your present and future relationship with the Inland Revenue before deciding whether any plan – including the one with monthly income – is likely to have an edge on net rates from banks and building societies.

Incidentally, the humble accounts at the post office, now known as National Savings ordinary/investment accounts, are good only for ease of access, although standing orders and bills can be paid this way.

The local post office also offers a way into government stocks, which are not to be confused with the bonds and certificates just mentioned. The mistake is easy, because they are dealt with centrally on the *National Savings Stock Register* whose office is near Blackpool. This place can buy and sell many (but not all) government stocks which are quoted on the Stock Exchange. The cost is less than going through a stockbroker, though it is slower and you cannot get a price in advance. The advantage of government stocks (known as gilt-edged) is that they too are guaranteed by the state. They are free of capital gains tax (CGT) and, if bought through the post office, the interest is paid gross. The best time to buy them is when the pound is weak, or interest rates generally are higher than normal, so they can be bought at a kind of discount. The grey form GS1 is for buying and the pink one GS3 is for selling. Fill them in at home and send in the pre-paid envelope to Blackpool. Leaflet DNS 708/85/01 or an updated version lists the latest stocks available.

ALTERNATIVE INVESTMENTS

There are a dozen other ways of investing funds instead of putting them in the bank, on the stock exchange or into property.

None of them is really for people of modest means, and even those with money to risk should beware. The commodities markets, e.g. sugar, coffee, cocoa, copper, tin etc. are for the experts and the rich. Recently there have been mailings by companies promising the chance to make a fortune on these markets. But bear in mind if those companies are confident they can do so, they would be borrowing money and making the profit for themselves rather than working for you. In the latter case they are sure to get their brokerage – win or lose.

The two-fold purpose of this section is to warn readers against the illusion of romantic riches whilst alerting those who may have hidden assets.

They may be in the form of gold or coins, silver or diamonds, wine or books, stamps or art, porcelain or furniture. Items like Georgian chairs have increased fivefold in value since 1975 while vintage claret has gone up eightfold in the same period. But the index of English coins has gone up only by a more modest 6 per cent.

The advantage of all such assests is that any disposed of for less than £3,000 do not attract capital gains tax (CGT) thanks to the so-called 'chattels exemption'. Their drawback is the risk of fire or theft, and so insurance cover will work out at around 0.2 per cent to 0.5 per cent.

Any such items that you have already, and have no wish to pass on to heirs, can be sold off periodically to make a useful extra top-up to your income. However, much depends on getting expert and honest valuations, and only connoisseurs or those with access to skilled advice should attempt to buy any one of the above categories (which once included whisky, and see how that has slumped!) For example, diamonds depend on cut, carat, colour and clarity – with the last two aspects now capable of being altered with lasers. Only the larger diamonds carry appreciable value and there has been a decline since 1980.

Only slightly better bets are gold and platinum ingots and coins, whose range has increased recently as Australia, America, Canada and the Isle of Man try to exploit the squeeze on the gold krugerrand. Various gold coins have different purity and premiums which can also depend on such factors as whether there is a queen's head. Prices are volatile, and anyway there is VAT in Britain and the Isle of Man, although this can be avoided by buying and storing with some bank such as Charterhouse in the Channel Islands.

If you are a speculator, good luck! Otherwise, the main thing about alternative investments is, find out whether you have some, then make a rough estimate of their value and keep quiet about it, although the insurance company should be told. It makes sense to take photographs of them and note any details along with approximate value. Some can be secretly marked with a UV pen (see page 192) but check first that you cannot damage the item, and mark it in an inconspicuous place.

DEATH AND PROVISION FOR HEIRS

Death may not be a pleasant subject, but it must be faced. It is only fair to your spouse or dependants to see that your affairs have been left as tidy and straightforward as possible.

Everyone should make a will, at any age, and keep it up to date, particularly if divorce or remarriage is involved.

Those with a clear head and simple instructions to give – such as leaving everything to the wife or husband – can doubtless save fees by writing a will with just the help of a book from the *Consumers' Association*. However, solicitors boast gleefully of how much money they make out of disputed or badly-drafted do-it-yourself wills.

Therefore it may be best to ask a lawyer, or maybe the bank, although their executorship may become costly compared with having this done by a nominated friend or kinsman.

The whole subject can be involved, so just note two more points:

1. The state gets the property of deceased persons who die intestate (i.e. no will) and have no close kinsfolk.
2. It is wise to insert the phrase, 'if he/she survives me by 30 days,' when leaving all to one's spouse, in case you are both fatally injured in the same accident.

As far as the funeral is concerned, a lot can be planned and saved beforehand by using a scheme by *Homeowners* or another friendly society which is tax efficient. Ask the *National Association of Funeral Directors* or *Chosen Heritage Ltd*. about arrangements pre-death.

For the surviving relative there is a lot of paperwork, so ask the DHSS for its leaflet *What to do after a death*. Form PR 48 explains how to get a grant of probate to approve the will. There are various books that guide you through the maze; the *Consumers' Association* publishes one and it might be well to have it on hand well before it is needed.

There is no death grant now but families on certain benefits will get some help for burial. The bank or building society of the deceased can release up to £1,500 on production of the death certificate, and joint accounts make things even simpler for a spouse.

The most sensible way is to have a special file in the desk at home setting out the steps which must be taken, from calling the doctor and clergyman to dealing with life policies and cashing in unused travel tickets.

Finally, do remember that in these days even assets of only £90,000 including the value of your home, car, furniture and other property plus savings, are enough to make your estate liable for inheritance tax (though not if all is left to the spouse). There are various schemes for avoiding this including a complicated one by *Touche, Remnant and Co*. together with the *Norwich Union Insurance Group*.

If you want to leave something to a charity ask its advice about how best to act.

Grandparents should consider covenanting now to youngsters with little or no income rather than leaving them money in the will, so that they can take advantage of any unused tax allowances.

FINANCES IN REDUNDANCY

There is probably more risk of redundancy in middle age than at any other period and that is certainly the time when it will cause most problems. You must take into consideration your change in status as regards national insurance and income tax.

The first point to remember when redundancy threatens is don't volunteer for it. The management may offer blandishments to make it seem an attractive proposition, but you may be in a stronger position to negotiate better terms if you sit tight and say nothing.

If redundancy is confirmed, you will be entitled to a certain statutory payment provided you have worked with the firm for two years for more than sixteen hours each week. If less than sixteen hours, you will have had to work with them for at least eight hours a week for the previous five years. In addition to redundancy payment, you should receive holiday-pay entitlements and pay during the notice period. It may be worth noting that if you take payment in lieu of notice, this is usually (but not always) paid free of tax depending on the precise wording of your contract of employment. As regards the leaving payment, the employer should be able to receive the tax inspector's agreement in advance on the tax treatment of an agreed sum, and this may obviate the necessity to reclaim a considerable amount of tax after the end of the tax year.

Failing that, large lump-sum leaving payments paid under PAYE during the tax year, particularly in the early part, would be taxed at an inordinately high rate.

If you belong to a union, it will almost certainly have agreed more advantageous terms than those laid down by legislation. In very general terms, you usually fare better if you work for a large firm than a small one.

There may be certain items you can negotiate, such as buying your company car at a favourable price.

The law relating to redundancy is complex, and in relation to any situation where you think you are about to be paid off, it is better to get legal advice before you take any action or agree to any compromises. However, it is very easy to throw good money after bad on an ineffectual solicitor as most will have had almost no firsthand experience in similar matters. It is preferable to go to a solicitor who customarily works for a trade union or who specialises in employment law.

Apart from the size of any redundancy or gratuitous payment, the pay-off normally should be free of all income tax up to a maximum of £25,000 and on a sliding scale thereafter.

After employment ceases you will then be entitled to unemployment benefit, but there are time limits. Another factor is that social security benefit may dwindle at age 60 in line with what one gets from an occupational pension from £35 weekly upwards.

RETIREMENT PENSION

Once you retire, it is vital to see that you receive all your entitlements from the state, your firm's pension and income from any other source, of which details have been explained in this chapter.

Remember, the amount you can earn before your state pension is affected is very low, in fact it is not worth earning much unless you plan to defer receiving the state pension for a year or so.

The limits usually rise yearly. The booklet *Your rights for pensioners*, published annually each July by *Age Concern* sets it all out in an easy-to-understand fashion. You can buy it from W. H. Smith and other leading bookstores or write to them.

If your state pension is virtually your sole source of income, it is even more important to ensure you receive any benefit going. The range is complicated – from supplementary benefit, help with fuel bills etc. You can get advice from the *Citizens' Advice Bureau* as well as the DHSS who have a range of leaflets explaining the benefits available. Ask the local council if you think you may be eligible for housing benefits or rates rebate. Age Concern has a wealth of helpful leaflets too – ask your local group. You should find them if you look in the telephone book under Age Concern or Old People's Welfare Council. The *National Consumer Council* can provide advice and helpful information.

YOUR HOUSING

Where to live has been discussed at length in a previous chapter but there are various financial considerations to bear in mind. As you get older there is a temptation to pay off the remaining mortgage. However, for reasons of tax relief (and potential social security eligibility) this desire for tidiness should be resisted.

There are other ways of using the value of your present house for income. Some building societies are starting to allow remortgaging by present members, up to a limit of perhaps two thirds of the property's current value. On death (or when moving) the building society moves in to sell the property and passes on any surplus to the owners or heirs.

Such schemes from building societies which have issued the original mortgage are likely to be cheaper than going to finance houses which specialise in remortgages.

Another variant of this is to sign over your home to a company which pays an income for it and allows you to become a lifetime tenant. Apart from the uncomfortable feeling, the danger here is that the company concerned could go bankrupt – so no more income and your home would be used to pay off its creditors.

There is a third kind of reversionary scheme, as they are

called. This one is part of a three-way link to provide the elderly person with a home and an income whilst avoiding inheritance tax by heirs. It is one of the options provided by *WICO/Hastings* of Farnham, which says the Inland Revenue cannot fault it.

Two final points should be noted about moving:

1. There has been a vast change in conveyancing and connected matters since many people took out their first mortgages many years ago. Cheap conveyancing and house purchase packaged paperwork are now coming in, so it is worthwhile shopping around.

2. The trend towards sheltered housing is a reassurance for those who are less mobile than they were. It is discussed in Chapter 5, Where Shall We Live? but for more details send for the booklet, A Buyer's Guide to Sheltered Housing, published by Age Concern or contact *Counsel and Care for the Elderly*.

ADDRESS LIST

Age Concern, Bernard Sunley House, 60 Pitcairn Road, Mitcham, Surrey CR4 3LL. 01 640 5431

Association of Investment Trust Companies, 16 Finsbury Circus, London EC2M 7JP. 01 628 0871

Building Society Shop, City House, Maid Marian Way, Nottingham NG1 6BH. 0602 472595

Chosen Heritage Ltd, Farringdon House, East Grinstead, W. Sussex RH19 1EW. 0342 312266; or Chosen Heritage, Freepost, East Grinstead RH19 1ZA

Citizens' Advice Bureau, see local telephone directory or National Association of Citizens' Advice Bureaux below

Counsel and Care for the Elderly, 131 Middlesex Street, London E1 7JF. 01 621 1624

Homeowners, Springfield Avenue, Harrogate HG1 5BR

M & G Securites Ltd, Unit Trusts, Three Quays, Tower Hill, London EC3 R6BQ. 01 626 4588

National Association of Citizens' Advice Bureaux, 115–123 Pentonville Road, London N1 9LZ. 01 833 2181

National Association of Funeral Directors, 57 Doughty Street, London WC1N 2NE. 01 242 9388

National Consumer Council, 20 Grosvenor Gardens, London SW1W 0DH. 01 730 3469

National Savings Stock Register, Bonds and Stocks Office, Blackpool FY3 9YP. 0253 66151

Norwich Union Insurance Group, 51 Fenchurch Street, London EC3M 3LA. 01 623 2575

Office of the Banking Ombudsman, 5–11 Fetter Lane, London EC4 1BR. 01 583 1395

Office of the Insurance Ombudsman, 31 Southampton Row, London WC1B 5HJ. 01 404 0591

Securities and Investments Board, 3 Royal Exchange Buildings, London EC3V 3NL. 01 283 2474

Stock Exchange, Thrognorton Street, London EC2N 1HP. 01 588 2355

Touche, Remnant and Co, Mermaid House, Puddle Dock, London EC4V 3AT. 01 236 6565

Unit Trust Association, 16 Finsbury Circus, London EC2M 7JP. 01 628 0871

WICO/Hastings, Clock House, Dogflud Road, Farnham, Surrey G09 70D

9
STYLISH WAYS TO SAVE

If you have changed your lifestyle in a pretty dramatic way, there's a fair chance you are living on less than you were.

Economy tips and ways of saving the odd pennies have a frugal ring, but in fact the operation can be quite fun. You can almost play a game with yourself in finding new ingenious ways to exploit your expertise in this field.

In ideal terms, you can save the pennies on things you don't feel too strongly about so that you can keep up to your previous spending level in other ways. Some are lucky and can cope with this formula quite easily, others have to be made of sterner stuff and tackle the problem on all fronts at once.

Most of us have some special weak spot, whether it is for Earl Grey in the afternoon or a liking for expensive shoes, or the stalls at the theatre rather than the upper circle. Even if you are saving your hard earned cash for these treats, or just to survive, there's no point in paying more than you have to for everyday goods and services.

CLOTHES

Look after the clothes you have and they will last longer. Always hang up trousers, jackets and skirts as soon as you take them off to allow the air to circulate around them and the creases to drop out. Close zips so that garments hang correctly and don't develop extra creases. Check for spot marks or sagging hems before you put them away and apply the appropriate remedial treatment. Stains dealt with early on are more likely to come out completely. Brush off dust, dirt or pet hairs so that clothes are clean while they are resting.

Apply the same treatment to shoes. Where possible buy 'good' shoes at the sales and they will last very much longer if you don't wear them on consecutive days. Give them a rest, on shoe-trees, in between. Clean them and give them a polish before you put them away as long as they are dry. If they are damp, allow to dry naturally. You can stuff the toes with newspaper to maintain shape.

To avoid shine on trousers and dark skirts sponge with warm water to which you have added a few drops of ammonia. Allow to hang out in the air to lose the smell.

When you buy a new garment, it pays to spend a little time reinforcing the thread on the buttons. You know how one pull and the whole thing disintegrates, and that means buttons are lost and you have to spend out on a whole set of new ones. Alternatively, the smallest dab of clear nail varnish will have a similar effect.

Now so many lovely clothes are washable, it pays to peer at the label before, not after, you buy. If you must buy clothes that will only dry clean, consider getting a load together then taking them to a coin-op dry-cleaner.

Don't throw any accessories away unless they are really decrepit. Good ones in the form of belts, scarves and bags will rejuvenate an outfit at no extra cost.

If you just get tired to death of a dress or a skirt swap it with someone of the same size for six months on the understanding that you will give each other the outfits back at the end of the time. You will find you welcome them back like old friends.

It is possible to make the most amazing savings by clever buying at jumble sales. Go for the basics like skirts and sweaters or blouses rather than suits that will probably be out of style.

Nearly New shops can be a good source of outfits. Though not as cheap as a jumble sale they will be about half the cost of those in the shops. It's a good way to get something for a special occasion.

People who make their own clothes save pounds, so if you like the idea, it's worth enrolling at a dressmaking class to learn how to do it properly. Buy your fabrics at the sales or in the markets and you will save even more.

The same thing applies to knitting. You can knit your own designer styles and save pounds. Buy the yarn in a sale or in the market. Sometimes you can unpick a sweater you have bought at a jumble sale or that you were thinking of throwing out. Steam the yarn so that the crinks drop out and start again.

Nylon tights can be made to last longer this way: before you wear them for the first time dip them in water, pop in a plastic bag and put them in the ice-tray of the fridge or your freezer. When they are frozen solid, allow to thaw and dry naturally.

Suede jackets or shoes can be revived by steaming them in front of a kettle or in the bathroom and brushing with a suede brush.

Remove the little fuzz balls from a sweater by shaving it very gently. Rub sticking zips with a lead pencil and always draw up the zip of any garment before you wash it.

Make sure you understand the care-code labels of clothes before you attempt to wash or iron them. It's only too easy to have a disaster with fabrics by treating them carelessly.

BEAUTY

Avoid the expensive though deliciously packaged creams and make-up. Ask for them as birthday and Christmas gifts instead.

Cream E45 made by Crookes is an excellent moisturiser and can be used for chaps and sunburn as well. It is usually on sale at the medicine counters in chemists.

Petroleum jelly used very sparingly makes a good eye-cream. Fingerprint it in very carefully around the socket of the eye, taking care not to drag the skin, and blot any residue away after about twenty minutes. It is also handy as a conditioner for eyelashes too and is soothing to dry lips.

A glycerine and rose-water mixture is a good all-round body lotion, although people with sensitive skins may find glycerine and witch-hazel more soothing. Use one quarter glycerine to three quarters witch-hazel and shake well before use.

To cope with dandruff, mix an equal quantity of cider

vinegar and water. Part the hair in half-inch gaps all over the scalp and apply the lotion with a cotton wool bud or cotton wool wrapped round an orange stick. Leave for a few hours, then shampoo.

Soothe rough hands by putting a teaspoon of granulated sugar with a little oil into the palm of your hand then wring your hands together and rub in the grains until they and the oil have disappeared. Pat hands dry.

Keep your mascara in a warm place and it will go further. When it eventually gives out, add a drop or two (no more) of water to extract the last from the tube.

Bottles of lotion or make-up will always go on for a little longer when they appear empty if you leave them upside down.

Use a lipbrush when applying lipstick. It will give your lips a much better outline and you will be able to get down to the very last in the tube. Wipe the brush clean after each use or you will end up always wearing the same indeterminate shade.

Look to products you have around the house that you can use to make your own simple skin products – eggs, honey, cider vinegar are just three ingredients that most people will have on hand. There are some first-class books around that tell you how to make up your own lotions – my favourite author is Clare Maxwell-Hudson – ask at your local book shop or the library.

SAVE ENERGY

Not running up large fuel bills while still keeping warm is the way most of us are looking to save money.

Look to your insulation for a start. See that your loft is insulated, your hot water tank has a good jacket – an 80 mm-thick lagging jacket is recommended by the Electricity Council. Lag hot-water pipes to maintain the heat and lag your cold pipes to prevent them freezing.

Check external doors and your windows for draughts, and take appropriate action. For internal doors you can consider a fabric 'sausage' if the draught still howls through. Cracks in floorboards can make it cold too if there is no carpet, so fill in any cracks that show with a filler of papier mâché which you can paint to the correct colour afterwards.

If you have central heating, turn down the thermostats and wear an extra woollie instead. One extra loose woollie is as good as a 2 °F rise in temperature. Close up rooms you don't use and turn the heating in them right down. Keep the doors closed so that the cold doesn't leak into the rest of the house.

Draw your curtains at night as soon as the temperature starts to fall. Well-lined curtains keep out a lot of cold, and you can try the insulated linings or use an interlining to make them extra snug.

Close off any unused fireplaces with hardboard but make sure you leave some ventilation. Never cover up ventilation bricks. Bathrooms, kitchens and any rooms where you use gas, bottled gas or paraffin heaters need adequate ventilation.

Save heating water by taking a shower instead of a bath where possible. Use the economy programme 'on your washing-machine and only wash when you have a full load.

Although you can save a little by turning off lights in the house when you don't need them, you can overdo it if you risk accidents by falling down the stairs or tripping in dimly lit passages. Dimmer switches can save on electricity, but of course you have to offset the cost of buying them in the first place.

You can save whilst cooking by always matching the pan to the ring size on your cooker. Make full use of the dual rings if you have them. Cook more than one vegetable in a pan if you can or steam the green vegetables over the boiling potatoes.

Aim to cook a complete meal in the oven when you have it on. Plan your menu so that you can cook the vegetables and a sweet all at once. When you cook a joint turn the oven off ten minutes early.

FOOD TIPS

Many older people have an in-built ability to budget for food, probably learned from their mothers during war.

They were brought up on the notion that they delayed their weekend shopping until late on Saturday night as the shops and the markets were closing and food that wouldn't last was sold off cheaply.

Refrigeration and deep-freezing has made such an opportunity less frequent, but it's still worth visiting markets as they begin to wind down and see if they have anything to offer. Soft fruit, tomatoes and mushrooms in particular are often available at a bargain price.

It is common sense to know exactly how your money is going so that you can take a fresh look at how you eat to see if improvements or simple cutbacks can be made.

Keep a detailed list of everything you buy for three or four weeks. Write it all down in a notebook. You may be astonished to see how much you spend on butter when you could substitute a mixture or go for margarine.

Frozen foods, although quick and convenient, are more expensive than fresh seasonal food. If time is not at a premium for you, there are obvious savings to be made in that direction.

Buy food in season when it is cheap – even short-season foods have a week or so when they are comparatively inexpensive. Buy fruit and vegetables mid-week and look out for pick-your-own farms, especially if you have a freezer.

Buying in bulk doesn't necessarily save you money. You should really do your own arithmetic and work it out for yourself. A tendency when faced with large packs of everything is to use a little more each time, so decant your dog meal or washing powder into normal-sized packs for regular use.

Food sold loose is generally cheaper than food sold extravagantly packed. Use screw-topped jars for your stores and find bright colourful labels for them.

Cut down a little on the amount of meat you use per portion and bulk up with lots of cheaper vegetables or pulses. Four ounces of meat per portion can be sufficient in these cases.

Get to know recipes for using cheaper cuts of meat and offal. A spiced pig's liver casserole can be delicious and is inexpensive. Chicken is a good-value meat but remember you buy it on the bone.

Buy bacon pieces in the shop and use them for savoury flans or for your bacon breakfasts.

Make a meal around canned pilchards or try sprats from the

fishmonger. Sprats are amazingly cheap and very tasty dry-fried and served with brown bread and butter.

Menu planning is important if you are really determined to stick to low-budget meals. Sit down and plan your food in advance, then shop for it a week at a time. Stick to your list and don't deviate. If you forget an ingredient, use a substitute so that you are not tempted by going to the shops too often.

Get into the habit of using herbs and spices – your own freshly grown if possible – to spice up your cooking. If you buy spices, get them from your local Indian corner shop where the reductions can be quite staggering.

Chutneys and pickles and ingredients like tomato purée also give a tasty lift to plain ingredients.

Use yogurt instead of cream – not only for health reasons but because it is so much cheaper. Get used to making your own in a vacuum jug or a special yogurt-maker if you have one.

Try growing your own sprouting beans or seeds on the kitchen window-sill – it's so easy and you don't have to wait long, just a few days, before you eat the results.

Make your own tasty stock every time you have meat bones available. Most of us have a chicken carcase every week or so and it doesn't take a minute to boil it up with a few herbs and let it simmer. You will find you get more flesh from the bones – enough for sandwiches all round – and you can keep the stock in your refrigerator, or for longer term, the deep-freeze, quite successfully. Bones can usually be boiled up at least twice whilst still retaining sufficient flavour.

The price of fish fluctuates, and unfortunately what used to be regarded as the cheaper end of the scale – delicious cod for example – is now pricey, but other fish such as coley and whiting have taken its place. Mackerel and herrings are usually cheaper and so are sprats.

Don't throw away dried-up cheese. It can be grated and stored in a plastic bag in the fridge for use in sandwiches or in cheese sauce.

Look in old wartime cookery books if you can find them in second-hand book shops or if you can borrow them from older relations – the austerity of those times brought out some very ingenious and money-saving ideas.

Making your own wine can become an absorbing hobby and can obviously save you pounds. Ingredients can be come by quite easily – in fact amateur wine-makers claim you can make wine from practically anything, including tea. The equipment is not expensive either; the refinements and special accessories can come later. Start with a prepared can of concentrate that makes it easy for you and then go on to find your own ingredients.

Fruit cordials can be made at home and will be more tasty than the bought varieties. They won't have such a long shelf life however, so make them little and often and store in the refrigerator.

FURNISHING TIPS

Stylish home-decorating needn't be expensive. A little imagination and the time to do your own work instead of employing other people can save you a great deal of cash.

The tip with decorating is to spend most of your time on the preparation. If you can't afford wallpaper, it makes sense to really fill each crack and smooth it with glass-paper before you apply emulsion. Work on the principle that if you can't disguise it, flaunt it for those quirks you can't cover up. Really ugly pipes may be disguised with a lavish hanging houseplant. A display of said plants in front of a badly plastered wall will detract from it. Well-placed lighting can lead people's glance away from the worn carpet and towards your favourite picture or the table beautifully laid for a meal.

Worn carpeting can sometimes be changed round or, alternatively, change the furniture around so that the worst of it is hidden. If your sofa has worn through its covering, disguise it with a patterned blanket or bedspread and bank it with a few exotic cushions.

When you need to replace expensive items like bedding, wait for the sales or consider making your own sheets and pillow-cases.

Look out for goods at an auction – it's great fun buying this way, as long as you can view the goods in advance and discipline yourself not to go over the top with your bidding. One answer is to ask a porter to do it for you – he will have a good idea how much the items will fetch, so his advice on the pricing will be pretty realistic and he will bid for you, although he will obviously expect a tip for this service.

You can often pick up items for a song by looking on the boards in newsagents' shops or the supermarket or the low-value columns in the local paper. Always make an offer for the items. You can always go back to the full asking price if you have to.

Remember that once you buy second-hand goods from a private person as opposed to a dealer, you have little protection under the Sale of Goods Act 1979. It is up to you to see that the goods are in order. Although a description of the goods has to be accurate, if the seller says nothing, he will not have contravened any laws.

Some dealers attempt to pass themselves off as private individuals to avoid coming under the act's jurisdiction.

Nevertheless, there are many excellent bargains to be found by buying second-hand, and it gives you a chance to go for better quality furniture.

Some items are offered at large discounts at certain times of the year from the high-volume furniture stores – look out for savings on kitchen units just before Christmas for example. Some of the out-of-town stores have sales throughout the year to clear old stock and savings can be made there too.

Window coverings can be an expensive item. Blinds are probably cheaper than curtains but don't have the same lush effect. The exception to this would be Roman blinds, those delicious horizontally pleated blinds made of fabric, or the very lavish Austrian blinds.

If you prefer curtaining, it is better to make lavish curtains out of a cheaper material than skimp and use something more expensive. Don't save money by leaving them unlined – they will never look the same.

If your house is double-glazed and not overlooked, you could consider not having a covering at all, though it may look bleak during the winter months. At the other end of the spectrum, thick curtains are marvellous for keeping out the draughts.

Substitute ingenuity for money when it comes to decorating. There are many beautiful books on the market that will show you how to stencil walls or floors, re-upholster a dining-chair or use découpage to give a new lease of life to an awful old chest of drawers. It's time that stops so many of us doing all these interesting things, and if it is what you have to spare, even if just for a short period, make the most of it.

ENTERTAINMENT

There is plenty going on around us to provide entertainment, so although it is nice to book expensive theatre seats or go to dinner at classy restaurants, it isn't strictly necessary to spend a lot.

In any town or village there is plenty of free entertainment. At its simplest you can sit in the park and watch couples playing tennis or go and cheer the local cricket team.

In summer any area is ablaze with open-air activities. There will be plenty of fêtes and you can spend a very pleasant hour or two at most of them without spending more than a few pence on the tombola or guessing how many currants in the cake. You may get an opportunity to watch a fun run or a pet show. You could discover a local arts and crafts exhibition – it's all good fun if you enter into the spirit of things.

At all times of the year you will find amateur dramatic societies and choirs in full flow, where for very little you can enjoy a good standard of entertainment at a fraction of the cost you would pay for a professional rendering.

Look out for lectures and discussion groups on subjects that interest you; political party events provoke a lively debate and you don't have to agree with their opinions to enjoy hearing their views or airing your own.

You'll find a lot of these events publicised in notices near car parks, local shops, the library notice board or any public notice boards as well as your local paper which you can usually read free in the library.

If you are eligible for a bus pass you can travel all round your area free, or at least at low cost. In London, for example, my mother used to travel literally miles and miles on the top of a double-decker and explore new aspects of the capital. British Rail offers fare reductions from time to time, so keep an eye open for their adverts. Your local radio station may organise events, so listen for news, and again, the BBC offers free tickets for some of its shows, so apply to them if you can get to the major cities and you will certainly have a wonderful time.

I personally find large garden centres a wonderful way of spending a pleasant hour or two. You can brush up on your knowledge of plants and see new varieties coming on to the market as well as enjoying the plants on display.

Don't forget that you can spend all day in the local library reading the papers or delving into the bookshelves.

Some evening or day-time classes are free to those who are currently unemployed or pensioners, or available at reduced rates, so it's worth enquiring about the situation in your area.

10
A CHANCE TO TRAVEL

This chapter was written with the assistance of Lynda Sebbage, travel agent.

One of the most exciting opportunities that more leisure brings must surely be the chance to travel. Whether you are between jobs, have taken a sabbatical or are experiencing retirement, the chance to take off appeals to most of us.

If your priority is to get back into the job market as quickly as possible, the best advice is to skip this chapter and refer to it at a later stage of your life. If, however, you have that niggling feeling that there is a great big wide world out there that you have yet to see, now is the chance.

Financial restrictions loom widely, of course, and whether you want to use up redundancy money on the holiday of a lifetime is a decision only you can make. Similarly if an insurance policy pays up, you may want to seize on the nest-egg and visit cousins in Australia or embark on a trek in the Himalayas.

Not all travel need be expensive. If you really have only a little money to spare, get to know your own country better, or take a coach trip to exotic foreign parts and be prepared to choose a different type of accommodation to keep costs down.

Be prepared to spend time reading up about where you plan to go. Imagine visiting Greek islands and missing a famous temple, or seeing the Taj Mahal before you know the wonderful story of why it was built. Remember that much of the pleasure of travel is in the anticipation, so take time to prepare your route, investigate the most suitable way to travel and find out all you can about the area before you start.

For some, travelling abroad can create problems of many kinds, and so travel is restricted to staying in the UK. However, you do not have to go abroad to enjoy a holiday – there is so much to see and do here. With such a varied choice at your fingertips you will not have a problem other than deciding where to go!

HOLIDAYS IN THE UNITED KINGDOM

Where?

Practically anywhere. From Scotland to Cornwall. If you are not sure, do make full use of the *Tourist Boards*. Each part of the United Kingdom has its own local or regional tourist board (see the Address List) which can deal with most enquiries. They will be happy to send you information which will help you plan your holiday. Before they can assist, however, they will need to know such details as when you can travel – off-season, mid-week etc, whether or not you are mobile, price range of your intended holiday.

Types of Accommodation

Depending upon your budget, the range is from guest houses or caravans to top quality, luxury hotels. For those who like to travel away regularly, and therefore are almost certainly budget-conscious, why not take a look at some of the holidays offered by *Saga Holidays*. To qualify for these you or your partner must be aged 60 or over. They offer very economical stays in universities at certain non-term times of the year, and prices include rail travel too.

Most popular tourist towns offer a wide selection of budget, privately run guest houses. For this information contact the local tourist board in the town concerned. Another excellent way is to rent a cottage or flat out of season. There are a number of publications which specialise in self-catering. Look for winter or cheaper months such as April/May and September/

October. With time on your side prices can be exceptionally low.

Although the weather will be more or less the same as it would be if you stayed at home, there is nothing like a change of scenery and a chance to get to know your own country.

Prices quoted in this country will not normally include the fare (unlike most foreign holiday brochures) so you will need to add this on when costing your break. Check, too, whether prices include bed linen and electricity. If you want to take your pet with you, again, check first, as the accommodation is usually privately owned and is subject to the owner's regulations.

Other UK Holidays

Coach tours are extremely popular, and ideal for single people as it gives them the opportunity to meet others. Most types of touring holiday collect from your nearest large town and so there is no hassle in making your way to an airport, particularly with all your luggage. Coach tours range from a weekend to eight days plus and operate all the year round, mainly to popular destinations such as the Lake District, Scotland, Devon and Cornwall and so on. Look out in your home area for any local firm that has its own programme.

Don't be put off coach holidays by thinking that you have to stay in a different hotel each night on top of spending all day travelling. Many of these holidays are based in one place – Eastbourne, Isle of Wight, for example. The advantage here is that the coach stays with you and is used for excursions and day trips.

Rail holidays are a popular way of travelling as they offer a fast, easy and comfortable way to reach your destination. British Rail has a number of schemes of which Rail Rovers, Local Rovers, a Freedom of Scotland ticket are just three examples. It is essential to read the leaflets carefully as they are full of ifs and buts, but they do offer considerable savings. From London, Intercity Savers offer an advantage if you can avoid travelling on Friday and pre-bank holidays. Don't forget the incentives offered by group travel. If ten or more of you travel together, one can go free. Look for the leaflet at your main line railway station or local travel agent.

It's Cheaper in a Group

Senior Citizens Railcards or Disabled Persons Railcards may have something to offer you. It's well worth looking at the leaflets available in the main railway booking-offices to see if there is a local scheme that could apply to you.

Golden Rail Holidays offer such a wide programme. They feature not only UK holidays, but foreign trips as well, and offer extremely competitive prices, staying in guest houses or hotels. Once you have arrived, there is nothing to stop you hiring a car so that you can be more independent.

All major car-hire groups have branches in large towns and can deliver directly to you if for any reason you are unable to pick up the vehicle yourself. A small charge may be made for the service. Always check for any special local promotional rates as each individual area has its own prices; of course, always check for those 'hidden extras' such as Collision Damage Waver (CDW) Insurance, Personal Accident Insurance, VAT and whether their rates include unlimited mileage. It always pays to shop around, but avoid going from one extreme to another and renting a doubtful vehicle that is likely to let you down or even worse, could be dangerous.

You will not need any documentation other than your current and clean drivers' licence – insurance documents are arranged separately by the car-hire rental company.

Short Breaks in the UK

These are a great way to spend a few days anywhere in the UK, and they don't have to be over a weekend – you can go during the week when it is quieter, although not necessarily cheaper.

First of all, it is important to decide on what you want from your short break. It may be to get away from it all, or maybe a shopping spree. Perhaps you could take the chance to join a special project such as a Bridge Weekend, Chocolate-making Weekend or one of the literally hundreds of other subjects to choose from – there are so many fascinating themes. You may be wanting that special break to celebrate an anniversary or a birthday.

Once your destination is chosen, decide on whether you need 'wheels'. Some towns are pretty isolated once you are there, but if it is a city where the major attractions are within walking distance, it is likely you will not want to drive once you are there. In that case, most mini-break tour operators offer excellent value-for-money breaks including first or second class rail travel from your home station at low add-on rail prices.

Many hotels cater extensively for the disabled, and those who would rather not leave their dogs behind in kennels can often take them along too – although this is obviously subject to individual hotel regulations.

Except for London, most short-break operators offer a fully inclusive price which covers accommodation, breakfast and evening meal plus service charge and VAT. (Rail-travel holidays, of course, include your return rail travel from home station.)

Prices at the time of writing (1987) start at £25 per person per night (excluding travel). It is worthwhile shopping around as some operators offer a discount for the quieter months of the year – January and February – which can be a good time to take advantage of a break when the sales are on and everything may seem a little flat after the excitement of Christmas.

HOLIDAYS ABROAD

Ferry Services

An excellent and often leisurely way to visit the continent is to take your car on one of the many ferry services which operate to and from various ports. Once over, you are free to plan your holiday as you like with complete flexibility and total freedom of the road. Make sure you invest in a good up-to-date road map.

Many ferry companies offer great winter reductions, and throughout the year will advertise special short-duration returns – 60-hour half-price returns, five-day returns and so on. Look out for the cheaper rates which apply to travel undertaken during the evening and early hours of the morning – it's surprising what you can save if you are willing to miss a night's sleep.

Big reductions are also offered for cars taking caravans or trailers at certain times, so it is worth spending time studying the various options open to you. Weigh up the advantages and disadvantanges of perhaps taking a cheaper crossing but adding more miles to your journey time – or it may be worth taking the longer sea route and letting the ferry company take the strain.

There are many routes to choose from, although most departure ports for Europe tend to be in the south of England. However, Hull and Felixstowe and Harwich on the eastern side of the country offer excellent and regular services mainly to Denmark, Sweden, Germany and Holland. Of course, from the western part of the UK there are services to Ireland, both south and north, and the Isle of Man. From Scotland, there is a network of small inter-island services connecting with the mainland.

When travelling abroad with your car, always ensure well before leaving home that you pack the essentials: car registration document (for Spain and Portugal check with the AA or RAC), warning triangle (compulsory in most countries) coupons for cheap petrol, available for eastern Europe, Italy and Yugoslavia (check with the relevant Tourist Boards), valid UK driver's licence (and for Spain and Italy you need a translation of same), International Driver's Licence for countries such as Spain (but check for up-to-date information with the AA or RAC).

It is important you contact your insurance company to arrange the car's insurance extension. They will issue a Green Card for a fee. However, if you are driving to Spain you may need a bail bond, so it would be wise to check well beforehand with your insurers. The full breakdown insurance offered by the RAC and AA for example, is well worth considering as they often give a 24-hour emergency and motor breakdown service.

You are advised to fit amber dippers on your headlights

when travelling in France, and in all countries to adjust the car's headlights to dip to the right. In some countries you must carry spare bulbs. Seat belts are compulsory in most countries and it is illegal for anyone under twelve years of age to sit in the front seat. It is compulsory for your car to display a GB sticker, which should be available free of charge from the ferry company or travel agent.

All these arrangements may sound like hard work but they are essential.

Long-stay Holidays

These are operated by a number of specialist and non-specialist tour operators who usually produce a separate brochure and market them towards the over-55s section of the community. The holidays tend to feature the major European destinations, particularly during the winter so that people may escape the harshness of Britain's winter for warmer climes.

For example, Spain, including the Canary Islands and Balearics, North Africa and the Algarve. The holidays are based on stays of two weeks plus. In fact many people stay for periods of three months or more. If they stay over Christmas, some operators will offer, at no extra cost, a free flight ticket home so that people can be with their families for Christmas. There is a choice of staying either in hotels or apartments and many fly from local departure airports.

Some operators offer 'theme' weeks for those with a special interest or hobby or wishing to learn one. Bowling, dancing, golf, photography, tennis, painting, walking – even keep fit. During the rest of the time, excursions and evenings out are arranged. You don't have to join in, but it's a good way to make new friends. There is no need to get bored, but it's always a good idea to have plenty of books with you and any easily portable hobbies – cards, tapestry, knitting etc.

This type of holiday can suit every kind of person, singles and couples, and many are ideal for the disabled too. Prices are excellent and when you work out the costs, they are truly amazing value. How can you stay at home for as little as £3 per night, especially in the bitter cold, when you could be making lots of friends in the warmth of Tenerife or Portugal? For Tour Operators to contact, see the Address List at the end of this chapter.

Winter and Summer Package Holidays

These are even more popular these days with an increased number of people taking continental holidays. When you have time on your side, the world is your oyster, and it does not need to be over-expensive either. The best advice is to shop around and steer clear of the busy high season dates when prices rocket.

What to look for:

Three weeks for the price of two

Selected holidays, particularly those to far-off destinations, offer this wonderful opportunity. Not everyone can take advantage of an extra week if perhaps they have only four weeks holiday a year, or their company may restrict the length of holiday taken at any one time. That is where you can benefit. Provided you travel within the set periods stated by the tour operator you will only pay for two weeks. However, in many cases, the extra week may be on a room-only basis – no meals included. Some holiday companies make it compulsory for you to purchase their half-board supplement although still allowing the third week's accommodation free. Always look at the prices first and do some cost-saving exercises. What may appear to be a wonderful offer may not necessarily turn out to be so.

Free car hire

This is available on selected dates and holidays. Once again, always check the fine details to see what you will be required to pay. The offer is good if you were going to need a car and it will save you some money, but otherwise it will add to your overall cost of the holiday.

Most major car-hire groups, such as *Avis* and *Hertz*, offer special discounted rates including unlimited mileage, if you book at least one week before the required rental date. Another good buy is that offered, for example, by *Pickfords Travel* and *Avis*, who run a 'Driveaway' cheques scheme. This operates in such a way that you purchase a required number of cheques, similar to traveller's cheques, from a *Pickfords Travel* shop. You do not need a reservation, as this scheme offers complete flexibility. You arrange your car hire when you reach your destination and feel ready to start exploring. The denominations of the cheques start at £13 per day inclusive of mileage, although local taxes and petrol, as usual, are extra. The price of the cheques depends on which country you are visiting, so enquire when making your booking. Buy six days rental and the seventh is free.

Free car parking

This can mean quite a saving if you are going to be away for a long time, or if you are often away, so look out for anyone offering this, or perhaps instead, free transportation to and from your local departure airport.

Single Specials

A major bone of contention are the sometimes rather heavy supplements payable on single-room occupancy. So look out for operators that in some rare cases do not charge a supplement, or maybe have particular holidays or departure dates with reduced supplements.

See the Address List at the end of the chapter.

Multi-centre holiday

If you are interested in long-haul destinations, always ask for a quotation to be worked out for you, as you can be independent and still take advantage of special rates offered in the brochure. All holiday companies contract out rooms at hotels which they use on their programmes, coupled with special air fares they buy in, so they can offer some extremely economical holidays to exotic destinations.

Don't assume this type of holiday is out of your reach. If you go in the low season and perhaps stay in a slightly lower-grade hotel, this type of holiday can compare with a typical European destination.

For example, look at this price comparison based on 1987 rates:

1. Thailand 2-centre holiday: 4 nights in Bangkok, Hotel Ambassador; 8 nights in Pattaya, Hotel Royal

Garden (room only, no meals). Including scheduled flights to and from London Heathrow during the period 8 April – 30 June. Price per person £579.

2. Gran Canaria single centre. 14 nights Hotel Tamarindos Sol. Bed and breakfast. Including charter flights to and from London Gatwick, June departure. Price per person £492.

One thing to bear in mind when considering long-haul holidays is that low-season prices may be because the weather is not so good – it may be the rainy season, or cold. So do ask your travel agent and be prepared to read some travel books yourself.

Free golf and / or water sports

Some hotels, through the tour operator, offer free use of their watersports facilities and some allow free membership to their golf courses. Always check whether that applies to you, especially if you are a keen sportsperson.

Complimentary lunch

This is available from selected hotels in specific destinations in which you are offered a complimentary lunch if you are staying at their hotel on a half-board basis during a selected time of the year.

All-inclusive holidays

Aren't they all? you may ask. Some hotels aim to include everything in the price. The Couples Hotel in St Lucia, for example, guarantees that everything is included in the price. The hotel will only accept bookings from partners of the opposite sex and no children or singles. You may or may not like the sound of this. It is aimed more at the younger set or at least 'young at heart'. It is certainly a popular choice and allows you the freedom of spending holiday money on other things.

Prices for this type of holiday include: full board, full breakfast, lunch and dinner; unlimited free bar with free wines, beer, spirits and cigarettes; free sailing, snorkelling, windsurfing, riding, use of Health Club, tennis, and free evening entertainment; free transfers from and to the airport, porterage, taxis and service charges – no tipping allowed!

When looking at this type of holiday always compare it with a similar one which does not offer all the 'free' incentives. Unless you are going to take advantage of all of them, you may pay over the odds and would be better to choose a conventional holiday where you pay for the extras as and when you use them.

Last-minute holidays

These are available all through the year, depending on demand. If holidays have sold well, particularly at their normal brochure prices, there will be fewer available at reduced prices. Most tour operators offer remaining holidays at lower prices approximately three to four weeks before departure. By that time they are prepared to cut their losses to ensure they have maximum capacity on their flights and in the hotels.

Shop around, but bear in mind these relevant points:

1. More often than not, you will not know where you are going to stay. Some operators will specify a grade of accommodation and perhaps advise the area you will stay in.

2. You cannot be too fussy. A cheaper last-minute holiday tends to be one perhaps no-one else wanted, and that is why it has been reduced. Alternatively, it may have been one of those elusive 'cancellations' that are returned to the tour operator for resale.

3. You will need to be flexible, particularly in the high-season time when space all round is at a premium. You may have to leave from an alternative departure airport and change your dates, perhaps even your preferred duration.

4. Be careful. Always book through a reputable travel agent and tour operator. Check they belong to the *Association of British Travel Agents (ABTA)* which will ensure your money is safe and which offers a conciliation service afterwards should you have any complaints that you have been unable to solve amicably.

Specialist Holidays

Golfing enthusiasts, for example, can book to one of the many famous golfing resorts through a specialist operator. There are many such companies catering for all interests from sailing to painting. Check with your travel agent who has a publication called *Who Goes Where, Doing What*, an invaluable source of information. Don't forget that many local groups and societies run their own excursions, but if they don't, it is always worthwhile suggesting they should start, as excellent group reductions will apply. All specialist tour operators are happy to give you further information and usually employ people with a good knowledge of that type of hobby or sporting pastime.

You can track down many specialist operators by looking in your particular hobby's magazines, or ask your travel agent.

Cruises

Perhaps a cruise would suit you. There are plenty to choose from, and once again, suitable for those with time on their hands. Cruises start from seven days upwards to several weeks, covering all corners of the globe.

Prices are relatively expensive, but as with all holidays, you do get what you pay for, and before you reject the idea, just weigh up what is included. No other type of holiday offers so much variety, visiting so many different countries on your floating hotel, with so many activities on board. There really is little time to be bored, and this type of holiday is ideal for singles and couples alike. Some cruise lines offer theme cruises – music, astronomy, gardening – you name it, it is possible they will have it on offer.

If you are unable to afford the full price of a cruise, and especially if it matters little when and where you go, *P&O Cruises* run a stand-by scheme, where if you register for a particular time, they will offer you a cabin at short notice, providing there is availability. The saving on this type of arrangement is marvellous, but you do have to be flexible and ready to travel at the last minute.

If you are in funds, the ultimate experience is on P&O's World Cruise, taking some three months to complete and visiting 21 countries around the world. Prices start at just under £5,000 per person for the complete voyage of 90 days. Expensive? That works out to be £55 per day and includes all meals. Large discounts are sometimes available if you settle your account early, so it is worth checking that with the cruise line. For other operators see the Address List at the end of the chapter.

Remember that to enjoy these cruises to the full other expenses are involved. You will want to build in on-shore excursions, you may need some new clothes, and spending money and tipping will take extra cash. *Cunard*'s QE2, for instance, will require you to 'dress up' most evenings.

Friends or Family Living Abroad

Friends or family living abroad provide the ideal excuse for travel. Very often it can be a daunting experience to journey to the other side of the world, when perhaps you are only used to travelling short distances, or you may not even have stepped on a plane before.

It need not be confusing or difficult to arrange, provided you find a professional and helpful travel agent who will discuss with you the best and, of course, the most economical way to travel. He will advise you regarding inoculations required and any visa documentation that may be necessary. If you require any special assistance, such as a wheelchair at the airport or special requirements in flight, all this can be arranged by your travel agent.

When you have made the final decision that you are going out for a holiday to perhaps Australia, New Zealand or South Africa or Canada, you will want to find the best, most economical way to get there. There are many different air fares available. The common rule is that the cheaper the fare the more restrictions it will have. For example, Apex fares are always purchased a set period of time before the travel date, and once you have made your booking it is unlikely that you will be able to change your reservation. All destinations have different fares, rules and regulations. Many large travel agencies have some excellent buys with some of the lesser known airlines which do not usually fly direct but via alternative intermediate destinations where you will have to change aircraft. It is important to weigh up the saving here. If you are saving a considerable sum over the normal, say, Apex fare, and do not mind taking longer to arrive, then it is a good buy. However, for first-time travellers or the nervous or disabled there is nothing to beat the direct service that avoids any change of aircraft.

Air fares are confusing, undoubtedly, but a word of warning – do not part with your money unless dealing with a reputable travel company who can give you a firm guarantee that your money is safe with them. Always be absolutely clear as to the cancellation charges applicable to your ticket and whether or not you are able to change it, either before you leave or whilst you are away. Most important of all, on all holidays, take out a full and adequate insurance cover with a cancellation section.

You do not necessarily have to stay the full time with your family and friends – indeed it can be a strain after a time, if you are going to be there for a number of weeks or even months. There are some excellent tours which you can pre-book before you leave the UK or once you arrive at your destination. The country's tourist board will be happy to provide the information.

Many airlines offer special visitor's fares for tourists originating in the UK. Australian domestic air fares are reduced by 30 per cent and American ones by some 40 per cent. Many major airlines operate promotional schemes on their domestic services in a bid to entice travellers to use their flights from here.

As regulations are changing all the time, it is advisable to check with your travel agent or airline direct for the most up-to-date information.

Not only do airlines offer reasonable flights, they can also book you a 'stop-over' holiday en route to your destination, particularly in the Far East which is a popular stop-over point for those travelling onwards to Australia. It can be a sensible idea to break a long journey say in Hong Kong, Bangkok or Singapore. Not only can it be arranged at a cheap rate – in some cases £20 per night – but it offers a superb opportunity for a little sight-seeing, duty-free shopping and a taste of the Orient too. Once again, see the Address List at the end of this chapter for suggested contacts.

Around-the-World Travel

Buying an around-the-world ticket isn't as expensive as it used to be. Most airlines offer attractive fares to enable nearly anyone to fulfil a lifetime's dream; but you do need to study carefully the various alternatives open to you.

Fares and routings vary tremendously and you need to work out first of all your proposed travel, then find an airline which works in conjunction with another carrier covering the routing in which you are interested. It really is the best way of visiting relatives and friends scattered all over the world, and of course, taking in the sights on the way.

You can travel First Class, Club Class or Economy, stopping over in a minimum of three places as a rule and taking between fourteen days and a year for the entire journey. As regulations stand at the moment, you need to book at least 21 days before departure and pre-reserve your first flight – thereafter you are flexible.

For a touch of class, maybe that really special occasion, why not travel by Concorde across the Atlantic and the rest by sub-sonic aircraft? One tour operator actually markets a round-the-world trip entirely by Concorde – perfect if you can afford it.

To get a clearer idea of how the scheme works, look at an example offered by *British Airways*. The world is 'cut in two' – northern hemisphere and southern hemisphere. Within each hemisphere you can select your route from a variety of possibilities.

For example, northern hemisphere covers the Middle East and Indian destinations, Hong Kong and Japan, returning through North America. At all times, travel must be in a continuous direction either eastbound or westbound. At the time of writing, the economy fare for this type of routing would be £1150 upwards to £2599 for First Class. Prices quoted are fares from London, and additional prices would be added on for regional airports.

The southern hemisphere, that is, points throughout the Far East, Australia, New Zealand, The Pacific and North America work out to be more expensive, which is hardly surprising when you think that down-under is included too! At 1987 prices you are looking at £1399 for Economy Class to £3400 for First Class.

There are a number of options available in addition to the standard fares. If you would like to deviate from the routings, most airlines will quote the extra price which usually works out just as favourable.

When you compare these with the normal fares and maybe even mile by mile, it's a pretty good way of spending a few months circumnavigating the globe in comfort. Don't forget, most airlines usually have some excellent discounted rates in hotels in all the points they visit, so you can have the whole tour arranged in advance to avoid any hassle. Many of the countries featured in the round-the-world routings do require that you are in possession of a valid visa and health certificate, so make sure you have this information well in advance of your booking. See the Address List for suggested contacts.

And Now for Something Different

There are less conventional yet still totally enjoyable holidays that may not be so well known.

How about a journey to the Caribbean by banana boat? A major grower of bananas in the Windward Isles of the Caribbean actually takes fare-paying passengers on its service to and from the UK. Reports claim that there is a high standard of accommodation and service on board. Bookings are restricted to only a handful of passengers and early booking is essential.

Time-sharing and villa-owning: much has been said in the media on time-sharing. It is essential that you are extremely cautious and check exactly what the contract means. It is also prudent to employ a local lawyer. Often you will find there are additional charges to meet each year, such as maintenance, membership fees and so on. You really would be well advised to weigh up if this is going to suit you and, of course, if you can, and do you want to afford it?

If you have the capital, you might be wiser to purchase your own property outright instead. This can be a great opportunity to get away from the winter cold and spend that time in your villa or apartment in the warm. When you are not using it yourself, you could let it either via an agent who specialises in such things or privately to friends. Even so, prudence is vital. To fly out, especially at the last minute, to any number of popular European resorts such as Malaga (Costa del Sol), Majorca, Ibiza, Minorca and so on, can be very reasonable indeed, especially during the low season, as long as you avoid periods such as Christmas, Easter and so on. Flight-only operators operate charter flights to the major resorts throughout the year from most British airports, and when they have spare seats at the last minute – a couple of days sometimes – will sell them off at prices that can even reach below £50. To save money but to book in advance you would be wise to travel on night flights – it is surprising how much cheaper this can be. Shop around for the best deal as they do vary enormously; but do ensure you make your booking through a reputable company.

If you are a keen sportsperson, there are many holiday companies which actually specialise in activity holidays. Trekking in the Himalayas if you are fit and a keen walker can be a fascinating experience. The average maximum walking period per day is only four to five hours, and you stay in tents en route. Luggage is carried for you by porters. There are safaris in Kenya and fishing holidays in Denmark, gourmet holidays in France and even in India. You can sample wine-tasting in Europe, or how about in Australia as an alternative?

You can try water-skiing, wind-surfing, tennis, golf, walking, skiing and even hang-gliding or hot-air ballooning.

For the keen sailor, whether experienced or never having sailed before, you can spend two weeks or longer learnig to sail around the Greek Islands and off Turkey's beautiful coastline. For more information, see the Address List.

With all these ideas for spending your spare time you may wonder how you will ever be able to afford it. Some people may be fortunate in having a healthy inflation-proof pension or other form of regular income, others may have an insurance policy about to mature, or decide to sell something of value to realise some cash.

Whatever your situation, there is usually a holiday that is affordable – particularly those long-stay bargains. Some travel agents offer a savings scheme which is worth considering. A number of retailers have incentives – £50 travel voucher if you buy their drink for example, or £25 off your next holiday if you collect a certain number of tokens. It is well worthwhile keeping a look-out in advertisements and on backs of food packets for incentives of this kind. But do read the small print every time as nothing is really given away, and you may find there are considerable restrictions before you can cash in.

HIDDEN EXTRAS

You may often be concerned that on top of the brochure price you could have lots of extras to add on – airport tax, insurance, surcharge, flight supplement, sea-view or meal supplements. On the whole, and at the time of writing, there is normally very little extra to be added to the final cost of your holiday. Make sure you study the prices carefully first and always ask your travel agent to work out a final costing. Prices in most brochures are broken up in departures in set periods of time – known as high, mid or low season. Prices vary within these categories. Either in the hotel description or above the relevant price panel, you will see whether the price includes any meals, ie. bed and breakfast, half board (dinner, bed and breakfast) (some hotels may offer lunch as an alternative, but normally dinner will prove to be better value) or full board. If the panel shows the price as bed and breakfast only, there will usually be a half-board supplement as an optional extra. In the description, note whether the rooms offer any facilities or whether these are extra. In self-catering, you will need to work out if there is an under-occupancy supplement, as this can affect the basic cost quite dramatically.

The brochure will also state whether there is a local departure airport supplement, as most prices are calculated from a central point. Airport tax in most cases has now been included in the brochure price.

Surcharges are few and far between at the moment, but always read the booking conditions which are, in fact, a contract between you and the operator. These have to state what their policy is regarding surcharges. Most often there is a maximum percentage on the total cost they may charge but it varies between operators. Weigh up the incentives offered for paying in full early to avoid surcharges. Would your money be better off earning interest in the building society perhaps?

Some tour operators actually reduce the prices of their holidays (known as relaunching) and if you have already booked you will feel somewhat aggrieved. Check with your travel agent as some operators would extend this benefit to early bookers.

Insurance is always an extra and must be something to budget for every time. Like holidays, you do get what you pay for, and the tour operator's cover does not necessarily have to be the best just because he happens to be selling it.

Read details thoroughly and compare various insurance offers. Pay particular attention to age limits, pre-existing illnesses and other clauses, such as how much is deducted as excess, and if they offer an emergency service to assist you wherever you are. Also, is medical cover as high as you can get? It is better to be over- rather than under-insured.

FINALLY

After making the decision to take those two months in Australia or three weeks in Majorca, how much do you need to save for spending money?

Some destinations are attractive in more ways than one, particularly if the cost of living is cheap. Nothing is more miserable than arriving and finding you are unable to relax and enjoy yourself because it is too expensive.

Most tourist boards will supply, along with the usual leaflets, a guide to the prices of drinks, meals, excursions and so on. Keep a close watch on exchange rates and the country's inflation levels. These are excellent indicators as to how far your money will go.

Firm favourites usually run year after year. Spain, Yugoslavia, Greece and, a relatively new recruit to the holiday market, Turkey. Further afield, India and parts of the Far East can be a good buy, but Japan is very expensive. The USA always has been popular with the British, offering a huge choice of holiday ideas, but the dollar against the pound has made it more expensive recently.

But wherever you go, prices of eating and drinking out vary enormously. Avoid famous landmarks and big hotels and you will find prices drop dramatically. Another tip is to eat and drink where the locals do – they are not going to pay over the odds and must know the best places. It really makes sense to get to know the local people. Language barriers permitting, they, of course, will always advise you to visit the best places and give first-hand advice.

Make the most of the enormous fund of knowledge a good travel agent has at his fingertips. Choose one who belongs to ABTA. He will have many trade publications and guides which are invaluable sources of information. One book in particular, available only to agents, will give forthright descriptions of some hotels, apartments and resorts which unfortunately the brochures all too often miss out.

Make full use of the tourist boards which can be found in London. You can either telephone, write to or visit them. Worth remembering is the World Travel Market held each year in late November at Olympia. Most of the tour operators, tourist boards, car-hire, ferry and shipping companies, plus many others are there and you will certainly come away with some excellent tips and advice. (Check which days it is open to the public.)

Possibly most important of all, take enough time to plan your trip, especially if it is beyond the sort of vacation you would normally consider. Make the most of the travellers' tales and guide books that you can borrow from your library so that you can get the feel of the country you are visiting.

When you plan the trip of a lifetime, start planning sufficiently far ahead so that you can choose exactly when you want to go without finding the flights are already booked as can often happen if you want to travel to Australia or New Zealand, for example, over Christmas or the new year.

The other reason for planning in advance, and possibly the

best of all, is that it can give you an extension of that delicious sense of adventure that any good holiday should conjure up.

ADDRESS LIST

Air New Zealand, 17th floor, New Zealand House, Haymarket, London SW1Y 4TE. 01 930 1088

Avis Rent-A-Car Ltd, 10th Floor, Hayes Gate House, Z7 Oxbridge Road, Hayes, Middx UB4 0JN. 01 848 8733

British Airways (specialist in all fares including round-the-world), Speedbird House, PO Box 10, London (Heathrow) Airport, Middx TW6 2JA. 01 897 4000

Cox and King Travel Ltd, 46 Marshall Street, London W1V 2PA. 01 439 3380

CTC Lines (Russian line), 1 Regent Street, London SW1Y 4NN. 01 930 5833

Cunard Line Ltd, 35 Pall Mall, London SW1Y 5LS. 01 491 3930

Danish Seaways, Scandinavia House, Parkeston Quay, Harwich, Essex CO12 4QG. 0255 554681

Falcon Holidays, 33 Notting Hill Gate, London W11 3JQ. 01 727 0232

Geest Line (banana boat), PO Box 20, Barry, South Glamorgan CF6 8E. 0446 732333

Golden Rail Holidays, PO Box 12, York, N. Yorks YO1 1YX. 0904 28992

Hertz, 1272 London Road, London SW16 4XW. 01 679 1799

Horizon Holidays, Broadway, Edgbaston Five Ways, Birmingham B15 1BB. 021 632 6282

Intasun Holidays Ltd (over 55s holidays, long-stay and general), Intasun House, 2 Cromwell Avenue, Bromley, Kent BR2 2AQ. 01 290 0511

Inter Home Ltd (house swaps), 383 Richmond Road, Twickenham TW1 2EF. 01 891 1292

Kuoni Travel, Kuoni House, Dorking, Surrey RH5 4AZ. 0306 888930

Longshot Golf Holidays, Meon House, College Street, Petersfield, Hants GU32 3JN. 0730 66561

Pickfords Travel Service Ltd, 400 Great Cambridge Road, Enfield, Middx EN1 3RZ. 01 366 1211

P&O Cruises – see Princess and Canberra below

Poundstretcher (flight-only specialist and part of British Airways, also do inclusive holidays and round the world etc), Airlink House, Hazelwick Avenue, Three Bridges, Crawley, W. Sussex CH10 1YS. 0293 518060

Princess and Canberra (P&O Cruises), 77 New Oxford Street, London WC1A 1PP. 01 831 1881

Qantas Airways Ltd, Qantas House, 395/403 King Street, London W6 9NJ. 01 748 3131

Rainbow Mini Breaks, Ryedale Building, Piccadilly, York, N. Yorks YO1 1PN. 0904 643355

Saga Holidays, Bouverie House, Middlesburg Square, Folkestone, Kent G20 1AZ. 0303 30030

Saga Holidays (cruises for over 60s), Enbrook House, Sandgate, Kent CT20 3SG. 0303 30030

Singapore Airlines, 580/586 Chiswick High Road, London W4 2PA. 01 439 3380

Sovereign Holidays, Room 430, Hodford House, 17/27 Hounslow High Street, Hounslow TW3 1TB. 01 572 7373

Tourist Boards
- English Tourist Board (also British Tourist Authority) Thames Tower, Blacks Road, London W9 9EL. 01 846 9000
- Jersey Tourist Information Office, Weighbridge, St Helier, Channel Islands. 0481 23552

- Guernsey Tourist Board, PO Box 23, States Office, Guernsey, Channel Islands. 0481 23552
- Wales Tourist Board, Brunel House, 2 Fitzalan Road, Cardiff CF2 1UY. 0222 499909
- Northern Ireland Tourist Board, River House, 48 High Street, Belfast BT1 2DS. 0232 246609
- Scottish Tourist Board, 23 Ravelston Terrace, Edinburgh EH4 3EU. 031 332 2433

TradeWinds Faraway Holidays Ltd, Station House, 10 Station Approach, Putney Bridge, London SW6 3UH. 01 731 8000

Wallace Arnold Tours Ltd, Gelderd Road, Leeds LS12 6DH. 0532 797755

11
YOUR SECURITY

Feeling safe is an essential part of enjoying life. It's miserable when you can't enjoy being at home in case you are burgled or are uneasy when you are out in case you get mugged.

It's an inescapable fact that it is necessary to take care and pay attention by applying common-sense precautions to look after yourself and guard your property.

Contrary to what is widely believed, older folk are not necessarily more likely to be victims of crime than anyone else, as long as they learn to be streetwise and avoid taking stupid risks.

PERSONAL SAFETY

Most of these suggestions apply to men and women equally, but women are more vulnerable in certain situations and need to be extra vigilant.

1. Avoid deserted or ill-lit streets at night and don't take any short cuts across waste ground or the park. Avoid alleyways where your exit could be blocked or where someone could lie in wait.

2. Don't walk too near the edge of the pavement. You could find that someone on a bike or even a skateboard could zoom by and snatch your bag. Face the oncoming traffic so that you can see who is approaching. It will also give you a chance to avoid kerb crawlers. It's as well to stick to the middle of the pavement as far as you can so that you are out of reach of

anyone standing in a doorway or obscured by a hedge or tree.

3. Stay alert as you walk, and don't mooch around or look lost. Try not to day-dream or dawdle. If a mugger is on the lookout for a victim, he is far more likely to avoid those who look as if they could look after themselves or are alert enough to scream and make a noise.

4. If you can avoid carrying a handbag at night, it is better to do so. Keep your money (and don't take more with you than you need) in a pocket or somewhere on your person. You could consider sewing a zipped pocket inside your coat.

5. When you carry a handbag keep it tightly under your arm rather than swinging free. This is particularly important on the underground or in crowded streets, markets for example. Choose a bag with a flap and interior zipped pockets so that even if anyone does reach inside, he or she won't be able to steal your wallet or purse. It is prudent, where possible, not to carry your credit cards and your cheque-book together in your bag. Don't carry house keys and any means of identifying yourself in the same place.

6. If you are coming home from an evening out, cover up any expensive-looking jewellery and turn any rings with stones to the inside of your finger, or even better, keep your gloves on.

7. Should you be attacked, it is better to part with your handbag or jewellery than risk injury. If you are merely threatened with attack, you may have a few vital seconds. If you can keep your mugger talking, you may be able to scream and attract attention, or even run away if there is any kind of help nearby. You may be able to fend off someone with an umbrella or your briefcase. It is possible to buy personal alarms, and if you have one, this could be activated. It is against the law to carry anything that could be termed an offensive weapon. Exactly what this might be is a little obscure, but generally, anything that you might normally carry about with you can be used to defend yourself.

Self-defence classes are often held locally, so it makes good sense to enquire at your local police station (ask for the Crime Prevention Officer) to see if there are any coming up soon. Your local Adult Education Centre may be running courses, too. Such classes are not just for the very fit and active but for people at all levels. It may not teach you to fight off an attack, but you will learn valuable avoiding techniques which could just give you those precious seconds to get away.

8. Being streetwise in a city means keeping alert to what is going on around you. You can often check whether anyone is following you by looking at reflections in shop windows. If you feel this may be happening, cross the road and see what happens. If you are still concerned, stop and ask someone for help or knock at the nearest house. If you see a crowd of yobbos ahead, don't ask for trouble by pushing past. Cross over the road or take other appropriate avoiding action.

TRAVELLING

Don't wait at lonely bus-stops at night, and never accept a lift, no matter how genuine the offer may sound. It is also sensible not to arrange to pick up mini-cabs in out-of-the-way areas.

Keep with people if you are waiting for a train, and if, when travelling, your carriage empties, move into another one that is still occupied. Women often feel safer if there are other women about.

Remember that any alcohol will affect your judgement, whether or not you are over the limit, and that it could impair your summary of situations and also of people. If you are at a party and have been drinking, ring a reputable company for a cab.

In the Car

Where possible, stick to well-lit and/or well-used roads. Don't park your car in an out-of-the-way place if you will be going back to it alone. If you are parked in a multi-storey car park, try and get someone to walk back to the car with you.

Keep your car keys in your pocket so that you don't have to stand and fumble in your bag at the last minute. Check the car before you get in to see there is no-one hiding – look behind the back seat.

Always keep your car, including the boot, locked at all times, even if you only leave the car for a few minutes.

188

Keep your handbag well out of sight, under a seat or in the front seat passenger well. It's only too easy for a cruising sneak-thief to grab the bag when you stop at traffic lights. The same applies to briefcases or parcels. Keep packages locked in the boot. Don't leave jackets hanging up in an unattended car.

Ensuring your car is well maintained will give peace of mind and the knowledge that you are less likely to find yourself stranded late at night. Always keep a can of petrol in a safety-approved portable container with you.

The police advise that you should think very seriously before stopping at what looks like an accident if you're travelling alone. Unless you have medical qualifications and could assist the victim, it is likely to be more helpful to drive on and report the accident from a telephone box or the nearest police station as soon as possible.

By keeping a map handy, plus a torch to help you read it, you are more self-sufficient in that you will not need to stop and ask for directions. It also makes sense to keep coins for parking or the telephone in the car so that you always have them ready in an emergency.

Even when your car is safely at home in the garage, avoid leaving the ignition keys in the lock. Don't keep your documents of ownership or insurance in the car.

Consider fitting an anti-theft device. There are many devices around now costing from a few pounds upwards. Some will be on sale at a good car-accessory shop. Some you can fit yourself and others will need to be done by an expert.

If you own a bicycle always lock it when you leave it, preferably to something permanent such as a lamppost. Make sure you have a description of your bike and note the cycle number. It makes sense to get it cycle coded (see page 192).

WITHIN THE HOME

Unless you are quite satisfied with the reason for their calling, don't let people into your home.

It makes sense to have a doorchain fitted and to slip it on when you are on your own in the house. Make sure that your door and door frame are sufficiently strong to stand the stress – it's no good fitting a chain if the wood is rotten or flimsy.

Crooks can be ingenious when it comes to gaining entry. One couple was attacked when bogus delivery men called to deliver a heavy parcel. A man may claim to be from the council or the water board.

Public service employees always carry an identity card and usually arrive in easily recognisable vans, so you should be able to check on them in this way. Take a good look at the identity card – they can be forged, and don't be too impressed by what looks like a uniform.

Other workmen from private firms will normally visit by appointment. If they don't, satisfy yourself that they are genuine. If you are doubtful, ask them to wait outside while you telephone the company. If they aren't genuine, this is usually enough to make them vanish. Even if you don't have a phone, you can still employ the same technique.

Some dealers seek to gain entry by offering to buy your furniture at a good price. They may offer what seems to be a lot of money for one item, only to trick you into selling cheaply something you may not realise is of value.

Beware of workmen who call to say your roof needs urgent repairs or who offer to tarmac your drive.

Most people assume that thieves are men, but this not so. The same advice applies to dealing with women and even young children too.

If something just feels wrong, play safe and refuse entry. Sometimes you can just sense tension in the air, in which case ask the caller to come back at another time. Should you be really worried, ring the police.

Keeping Burglars Out

Anyone living alone should be extra vigilant, and women should avoid displaying their full names either on plaques or doorbells – just use initials and surname only. In the telephone directory, stick to the same formula.

Take care of your doorkeys. When you move to a new home,

change the locks. Don't leave spare keys in obvious places – it is safer to leave an unmarked key with a neighbour than to leave one outside the house. However ingenious you think the hiding place, a burglar will have seen it before. Be discriminating about giving a key to anyone else – it doesn't take long to get one copied.

Don't make it obvious that you are not at home by leaving notes pinned on the door or the garage door open.

Check all doors and windows are shut every time you go out – thieves have been know to slip in while you are chatting to a neighbour or tidying up the garden. If you are tempted to leave a window open for the cat, find another way for moggie to enter. Even upstairs windows can be entered pretty easily, especially if you leave ladders in the garage or they are sited near a flat roof or a drain pipe.

Most thieves make their entry through insecure windows and doors, so the first task is to ensure that your back and front doors are as secure as possible. Fit all outside doors with a good quality lock – preferably a deadlock type, which is one with a bolt that cannot be retracted without using the key. Look for one with a British Standard Kitemark. Put bolts at the top and bottom as well, and use them.

Use appropriate window locks for all windows downstairs and any that are easily accessible upstairs.

Avoid keeping cash in the house – it's safer in the bank or post office.

When you go out at night, leave lights on – not just in the hall but in a room as well. Consider investing in a time-switch so that the light can be switched on and off in your absence. There are other sophisticated devices whereby lights will switch on at dusk by means of a sensor.

Where possible, have a light over your porch so that no-one can hide and rush you as you open your front door. For the same reason, it's a good idea not to have too many bushes or trees close to the house.

If you return home and think there may be intruders, don't consider confronting them. Drive on to a neighbour and phone the police from there.

MARKING YOUR PROPERTY

Coding your property doesn't just apply to precious silver or valuable antiques, it can apply to anything you value, and that must mean most things you have worked so hard to buy – like televisions, hi-fis, video recorders, ornaments and household appliances.

It can be useful to code-mark garden mowers, tools and, of course, your car or motor cycle or the bike.

Items, including clothes, can be marked in varying ways, and it can be visible or hidden. The three methods are engraving, ultraviolet (UV) marking and punching. The general way it works is to use your postcode followed by your house or flat number or the first two letters of the name of your house. If you move, you just place an X at the end of the old post code and mark again with your new one.

Engraving and punching is permanent and can be used on those items which will not be damaged. For antiques or other precious goods that would spoil, you can use a UV marker. With these, the fluid is visible until it dries, after which it can be detected by means of an ultraviolet lamp. This form of marking can be affected by dry-cleaning.

There are do-it-yourself kits available which contain stickers which warn that property has been marked. One in the window at home or displayed in the car should deter opportunist thieves. Police also claim that it makes a dramatic difference to enabling them to restore property to owners should it be stolen.

Advice on all forms of security is free from your local Crime Prevention Officer who will visit your home and tell you how best to protect it.

12

BEING ALONE

If you have spent your life surrounded by people at home, it can come as a devastating shock to be faced, possibly suddenly, with only your own company. However much you may come to enjoy it – and many people do – it does take some getting used to, and depending on your circumstances, there may be years in between when you feel overwhelmed and depressed, lonely and hard-up.

Supposing it has been your resolution to go it alone. You may have found that your aging parents you have stayed on to look after can manage for themselves or have gone into sheltered housing. Perhaps you have been bringing up children and they have left home. You may have decided to leave your partner and taken a sort of voluntary decision to find a flat. In all these circumstances you may feel it should be comparatively easy to adapt. Perhaps for you it will be, but don't be surprised if it takes far longer than you expected.

If you have lived all your life in your parents' home, you will have been very dependent on them in the past when you were younger. Even now the roles have been reversed, you will still find that you have depended on them for company and for emotional support and as a reason for being.

Children leaving home can have a catastrophic effect on any parent, particularly a mother, and if you are now without a partner to whom you can voice such feelings, life can seem barren.

Taking the decision to leave a partner and go it alone means you have a lot of courage to face facts, but it is a lonely choice that may meet with disapproval from friends and relations. At best you will be facing a drop in your living standards and the loss of some mutual friends.

These reasons for finding oneself alone are generally premeditated, so that however fundamentally different you will find life from now on, there isn't the added sense of shock that can come if you are faced with bereavement or when a partner suddenly announces that he or she is leaving and your life together is over.

In the case of bereavement, whether or not it was unexpected, there is still the state of total shock. People who have experienced this, explain that their feelings for some days are quite numb. It is not unusual for them to go about their daily tasks almost as if nothing has happened. During those early days there are many practical matters to attend to, and friends and close relatives usually rally round to offer practical help and comfort.

In the case of being deserted there is no automatic standard of behaviour that one can adopt. There is a lack of accepted social procedure that makes the situation more difficult. One thing is certain: in addition to the shock and outrage you may feel, you will also suffer bitterness and anger. Anger that this has happened to you, especially if you have been deceived and there is 'an other' on the sidelines. You will probably feel a deep sense of failure, that you are worthless and that you don't deserve to be loved. These feelings will pass as you gradually build up new ground, but they will cause you to feel deeply depressed at various times.

What is important throughout this voyage of self-discovery is to realise that they are phases, most of them a necessary part of coming to terms with your new life. You may not be able to avoid such distress, but if you can recognise that you will come through before too long, it will be easier to face.

TAKE STOCK

Two critical decisions may have to be made before you are really in the proper frame of mind to make them. One will be to work out how you can manage financially and the other is whether you should move.

Moving house has been widely discussed in Chapter 5, but the important fact about moving following bereavement or divorce is not to do anything in too much of a hurry. Most counsellors advise leaving any irrevocable decision for six months. This may be more easily said than done if lack of finances is a pressing point.

Managing money, discussed in Chapter 8, emphasises the vital point of ensuring you get all your state benefits. In the case of bereavement there is a range of benefits for which you can apply. Your local DHSS office can give advice, but the facts are usually set out clearly in a leaflet and it is probably better to read that carefully, so that when you go along to the DHSS you have a list of specific questions to ask them. Failing that, contact your local Citizens' Advice Bureau.

It is important, as far as possible, to think calmly about what you are going to do in the future. The decisions you make will have far-reaching effects, and it is only too easy to jump to on-the-spot conclusions based on emotion or irrational judgement that may have to be undone at a later date.

Avoid taking a decision that might involve selling your home and moving in with a relative or friend. Your own possessions, and even the knowledge that you are staying on in the home you have loved, may prove to be the lifeline you need for future days. If, after six months or so, you still decide you should make a change, you will at least have based it on more dispassionate grounds.

Early on you will need to work out a realistic budget. Make sure that you are claiming all your entitlements including maintenance, if divorce is involved and it is part of your agreement, or, in the case of the death of your partner, any insurance payments or pensions that may be due to you. It is also essential to check that there are no debts outstanding or, if there are, to make arrangements to pay them as soon as possible.

If your partner has died, you may be entitled to a firm's pension, or to cash in insurance policies. You should have a document listing all the assets, including bank accounts, credit cards, insurance policies and whom to contact regarding pensions and any other entitlements. It makes such sense to have such a document in a safe place that it is astonishing that so few people take the time and trouble to provide such a list.

Your next task will be to find out exactly how much you spend over the year. Go through past cheque books, bank accounts etc. to assess what your outgoings are. Include such items as the car tax and general maintenance, as well as any sum you may need to keep up your home, decorating etc. You may find this is difficult if you, as a wife, have always left this to your husband and just managed the housekeeping side of the budget. Similarly, a man may have little idea of food and dry-cleaning costs etc. But the sooner you can get to grips and discover the total picture, the sooner you will be on the long road to independence. Include yearly expenses such as (hopefully) a holiday, birthday and Christmas presents, once-a-year insurance payments and so on. Unfortunately, the magic figure of income and expenditure rarely match up, let alone leave you anything for future savings.

Now is the time to sit down and work out what savings can be made in your day-to-day running expenses. Sometimes just saving a sum off each major item, more chicken less rump steak, growing your own vegetables instead of buying them for example, or turning the heating down two degrees and wearing an extra jumper can all help. The savings will by no means be spectacular, but if you cut a little off everything, you may be pleasantly surprised. Can you raise some extra money by taking a part-time job, having a bed-and-breakfast lodger or doing more maintenance jobs around the house yourself instead of calling someone in to do them for you?

You may find it prudent to arrange with the bank to have a budget account to cope with big bills arriving all at once and ahead of your income. Check the charge the bank makes.

If you are temporarily short of money while you get yourself sorted out, you could have a word with the building society if you have difficulty in meeting mortgage repayments. Discuss the overall position with your bank manager. If you are really out of any form of cash, you may be entitled to state benefits – ask the DHSS or get help from the Citizens' Advice

Bureau. However short of cash you are, don't be tempted to go to a commercial loan company. The APR rates are extremely high and you will find it increasingly difficult to extricate yourself.

PRACTICAL MATTERS

Men and women will both have some adapting to do if they are faced with doing everything for themselves instead of being able to rely on another half.

Women will probably find the replacing of fuses and mending the electric kettle an unfamiliar pastime, and men may find it vexing to cope with the ironing or cooking on a regular day-to-day basis.

Although neighbours and friends will be helpful, it is a great mistake to expect to rely on them too much. If a woman is perpetually asking a neighbour's husband to help her with such tasks, she will soon put a severe strain on the relationship.

If you have really never learned simple tasks like changing a plug, the only recourse is to find out how as fast as possible. You can learn much from books, but where electricity is involved, check that you have understood the instructions by doing it in front of a friend who knows the ropes before you put it into practice. After the initial frustration, you will find it encouraging that you can do these jobs for yourself.

Men who find household chores difficult to cope with can take their washing to the launderette for a few weeks while they learn the ropes, and either forget the ironing or just run over what is essential. Preparing meals can be dealt with by using simple dishes that need virtually no preparation, but avoid ready-prepared frozen meals which can be expensive. It may be fun to join a cookery class at an evening institute – you will be warmly welcomed and have a chance to ask all sorts of questions as well as add to your recipe repertoire.

Both sexes can be pretty ignorant about car maintenance, which is more difficult to deal with. It isn't too much at least to see you know how to check the oil and tyre pressures and are prepared for the days when the car is difficult to start by arming yourself with such items as Damp Start and getting to understand the foibles of your own particular engine.

You can find a number of helpful aids for normal maintenance at a good car-accessory shop. Look out for rust and deal with it as soon as you can. Keep your car serviced regularly and keep your car manual in a safe place so that you can refer to it quickly.

You will find that if you can attend to practical matters easily, it will make day-to-day living much less stressful and you can concentrate on the more complex emotional problems.

You cannot avoid feeling upset and depressed, so don't feel you are a failure if there are days when you fear you cannot cope. It helps to have a friend who is willing to listen while you spill out your thoughts – such confidants are rather thin on the ground, but those who have trodden the same path already will know what you are going through. It doesn't do to bottle everything up in the great pretence that everything is normal, so don't try. Don't attempt to save your children by always appearing as if everything were normal. Family can be the greatest comfort of all as long as you don't expect from them a maturity and understanding beyond their years.

NEW SOCIAL LIFE

When you are solo once more after being part of a couple it will change your social life, and there is little point in pretending it won't.

Depending on your previous activities, it may be obvious or more subtle. With the best will in the world, couples will hesitate to invite a single person to their dinner-parties or invite them to share their holiday. There are several reasons – they may feel awkward, they may feel it isn't a good idea to make up odd numbers, and one partner may feel that you are now a potential rival. On the whole, men fare better in this dilemma than women because most couples have single women friends who can be invited to make up the numbers while single men past a certain age are rarer birds.

Sometimes it helps if you take the initiative yourself. If you previously invited friends around to Sunday lunch go on doing so. Get a friend to help you pour the drinks or serve the meal.

As a woman, you are more likely to find that you are invited back to all-women gatherings.

The looser network you have as a social life will probably serve you better. If you belong to an association with a purpose – an amenity group, a political association or a rambling club, you will find plenty of companionship on hand, particularly if you can be useful, possibly by offering to do some of the less popular jobs. Evening classes or local clubs may be full of women in similar circumstances to yours and will quickly offer friendship.

Some folk need people around them more than others, and on this depends how you can build up your new life. If you were in the habit of holidaying with friends and going out to the pub or to eat regularly with your own intimate crowd, it will take longer to fill the gaps. It isn't much good harbouring grudges if you are no longer invited as often unless you want to lose the friendships for all time. Even the warmest-hearted friends may now be at a loss as to how to deal with the new situation.

If you find certain places or situations bring back unhappy memories or tear-jerking happy ones – perhaps it would be better to avoid them for a while until you feel more able to tackle the problem. If you find that a particular time of day or the weekend makes you feel low, take active steps to keep busy at those periods, or find a new activity that requires you to be somewhere else.

Many people newly on their own find Saturday a particularly troublesome day, because they seem to be surrounded by busy, apparently happy families with things to do and places to go. It can be a problem when everyone else seems to be enjoying leisure time and you have nothing special to do. The answer is to save a particular treat for that day, or join a club that meets on a Saturday, or go and help out somewhere where Saturday is a busy time.

One thing is certain, you will never meet other people if you stay at home. Isolation is the biggest enemy of beating your loneliness. We may not all have a wide network of friends, but you can increase your circle by going out and about. If you feel like going out every evening, do so. It can't do any harm and you can always make up time for chores at the weekends or in the early morning. The more you are involved in outside activities the bigger your chance of making new friends.

Making new friends will take time. Don't expect to go out one day and come back with one as you would a trophy. Be content to build up acquaintances and then wait and see what happens. Don't try too hard or you will put others off. If you seem too anxious, they may feel that they may not be able to cope with your demands. Take it a step at a time and build up a friendship slowly.

Sometimes you may feel you are up against a brick wall. Your overtures are rebuffed, no-one wants to pass the time of day, or you sit on your own at a coffee morning. Don't despair. It isn't treatment meted out especially to you. It can happen to everyone at some stage. The remedy is not to waste your time pursuing a camaraderie that isn't there, but to move on to something more fruitful.

Lack of confidence or the feeling that you are rather dull may be a difficulty you face. If you have spent years involved solely with domestic activities, have held down a boring job and had little time to take up special interests, you may think you have little to interest others. Remember they may well feel the same. You don't have to engage in meaningful intellectual discussions from the beginning, in fact it would be off-putting if you were to try. There is time for that later on. Be yourself, be prepared to listen and be interested in what is going on around you. There isn't such a thing as a boring person – it is only a question of discovering their particular interest.

NEW PARTNERS

Ideally, making friends should involve both sexes – sometimes this happens as a matter of course, but very often it doesn't. It is undoubtedly easier for a man to take up friendships with women than vice versa, principally because there are more available women.

Both men and women should beware of taking up with a partner for the wrong reasons, such as the chance of financial security or to alleviate loneliness. It is easy to seize on the chance of a relationship as the cure-all, but the greater the problem the less likely it is to be an answer.

Take friendship slowly and don't rush into a sexual relationship unless you really want to. It can be extremely difficult to set about 'dating' again after many years, and it is all too easy to rush into having sex because you feel it is required of you and is the 'norm'. The only way to cope is to rely on your own gut-feeling, but saying no could be very much easier than getting involved more than you really want to and having to extricate yourself later.

13

TEN-POINT CHECKLIST FOR CHANGE

Everyone has his or her own way of coping with changes in life. Some manage better than others. Here is a checklist.

1. Accept that change is an inevitable part of life. There is no way of escaping it and we shouldn't want to. For every step back there can be two forward if you can view things in a positive way.

2. No change is wholly good or bad. There will be elements of both in every situation. Even if you were left a million pounds, there would be the worry of how to look after it. If you get promoted and it means moving, you may miss your old friends or find responsibility hard to take. On the other hand, you can retain your old companions and make new friends as well, and get to enjoy the stimulus of extra responsibilities.

3. You will cope with the ups and downs of life far better if you are fit. Even if you have managed to evade the barrage of advice that is handed out from every source, you must know it makes sense. Maintaining sensible weight levels and embarking on a fitness programme will give you added energy and enthusiasm for life.

4. Although you cannot turn back the clock, you can look attractive at any age, if you take care of yourself. Learn to accentuate your plus points and play down less good ones. Don't waste time trying to alter what cannot be changed, but concentrate on what can and should.

5. If you are interested in what is going on around you, you will in turn be interesting to others. There is nothing like enthusiasm to enliven your life and those nearby. Even the housebound can keep active minds and consider studying or taking up sedentary hobbies.

6. You will be in a position to enjoy change far more if you can cope with the financial ups and downs. Control your finances; don't allow them to control you. Easier said than done, but be aware of how much you spend, and how it is allocated, then if you have to pull back, you will know roughly in which direction. Keep abreast of financial changes that are going on all the time – new state benefits, extra incentives from the bank, special offers that might be just what you are looking for.

7. Where possible, plan for major changes in your life – retirement for example. Don't act as if it only happens to others. By planning far ahead, perhaps re-emphasising your interests and hobbies beyond work and entering into local community life, you can come into one of the happiest phases in your life.

8. As far as you can, keep a wide network of acquaintances and friends. You will find it stands you in good stead. Aim to have friends of all ages. Keeping up with everyone takes time and effort, and it is possible you won't really appreciate them until adversity strikes or you need a helping hand. Make certain that you are as good a friend/neighbour to others as you would like them to be to you.

9. If for any reason you are forced into rethinking your lifestyle, see it as an adventure – a great joyous step into the unknown. People who can see change in this way are invariably the ones who get the most out of it.

10. Don't look back – at least not often. Regrets and too much nostalgia have a stifling effect on what is going on today. What's done is done – you cannot change it, so as far as possible, look forward with zest and enthusiasm for the good times ahead.

Index

NON FICTION AVAILABLE FROM PATHWAY

The prices shown below were correct at the time of going to press. However Transworld Publishers reserve the right to show new retail prices on covers which may differ from those previously advertised in the text or elsewhere.

☐	17275 1	**MAKING LOVE DURING PREGNANCY**		
			Elizabeth Bing & Libby Colman	£3.50
☐	12815 5	**THE HEADACHE AND MIGRAINE HANDBOOK**	*J. N. Blau*	£3.50
☐	12734 5	**THE PATIENT'S COMPANION**	*Vernon Coleman*	£3.95
☐	99238 0	**ADDICTS AND ADDICTIONS**	*Vernon Coleman*	£3.50
☐	17356 1	**RUNNING WITHOUT FEAR**	*Kenneth Cooper*	£3.95
☐	12798 1	**THE BITTER PILL**	*Dr. Ellen Grant*	£3.50
☐	99242 9	**JUDITH HANN'S TOTAL HEALTH PLAN**	*Judith Hann*	£2.95
☐	99246 1	**COMING TO TERMS**	*Roberta Israeloff*	£3.50
☐	17362 6	**RECIPES FOR ALLERGICS**	*Billie Little*	£3.95
☐	17274 3	**RECIPES FOR DIABETICS**	*Billie Little & Penny L. Thorup*	£3.95
☐	17273 5	**THE HERB BOOK**	*John Lust*	£4.95
☐	99244 5	**HOMEOPATHIC MEDICINE AT HOME**		
			Maesimund B. Panos & Jane Heimlich	£4.95
☐	12829 5	**THE A FOR ALLERGY DIET**	*Barbara Paterson*	£2.95
☐	12822 8	**NEW WAYS TO LOWER YOUR BLOOD PRESSURE**		
			Claire Safran	£3.95
☐	17272 7	**GETTING WELL AGAIN**	*Carl & Stephanie Simonton*	£3.95
☐	99263 1	**LEARNING TO LIVE WITH DIABETES**	*Dr. R. M. Youngson*	£3.50

ORDER FORM

All Corgi/Bantam Books are available at your bookshop or newsagent, or can be ordered direct from the following address:

    Corgi/Bantam Books,
    Cash Sales Department,
    P.O. Box 11, Falmouth, Cornwall TR10 9EN.

Please send a cheque or postal order (no currency) and allow 60p for postage and packing for the first book plus 25p for the second book and 15p for each additional book ordered up to a maximum charge of £1.90 in UK.

B.F.P.O. customers please allow 60p for the first book, 25p for the second book plus 15p per copy for the next 7 books, thereafter 9p per book.

Overseas customers, including Eire, please allow £1.25 for postage and packing for the first book, 75p for the second book, and 28p for each subsequent title ordered.

NAME (Block Letters)..

ADDRESS ....

....